The Golden Thread
Spiritual and Mental Health

Rev. Geoffrey S. Childs

Assisted by Heather Childs
Illustrations by Karen C. Elder
Diagrams by David E. Childs

General Church Publication Committee
Bryn Athyn, Pennsylvania

First edition

ISBN 0-910557-15-2

Printed by General Church Press
Bryn Athyn, Pennsylvania
United States of America

1986

Dedication

to Helga

Acknowledgments

I would like to express gratitude and appreciation to reviewers of the draft manuscript who gave invaluable advice and counsel: the Rev. Walter Orthwein III, Sarah Headsten, the Rev. Donald Rose and Dr. James Pendleton. Each in different ways contributed comments and suggestions that were of strong help and in my opinion added to the worth of the book. Also, I would like to thank Dr. Basil Orchard for general counsel.

I would also like to thank David Childs for his graphs and diagrams of certain technical parts, and Karen Childs Elder for her drawings portraying essential values.

Without Heather Childs as an editor, expediter, critic and at times co-author, this book would probably never have been written, or would not have been written with the same clarity.

I would like to give special thanks to Sarah Headsten, Warren David and John Raymond for their willingness to proofread and correct the final draft of the manuscript. Finally, there is my deeply felt appreciation of the counsel and support of the General Church Publication Committee, and especially its Chairman, the Rev. Lorentz Soneson.

Contents

Preface

In a discussion I once attended at a mental health seminar, a sharp difference of interest became apparent in the group. We were talking about the relationship between mental health and religion. Some of the group wanted to discuss only doctrinal principles, searching for revealed truths that would shed light on the subject. They were, perhaps, unwilling to face a truth inherent in the subject: the terrible agony of emotional illness. Others in the group, perhaps overreacting, wanted instead to "get at what we really feel," to talk about "gut" feelings instead of abstract doctrine. They did not reject doctrine, but it was not their present concern; the desire to get at feelings resulted from a freeing-up of blocked emotions that these people had recently experienced.

The danger in this discussion group was the either/or conundrum: either doctrine or feelings, but not both. Yet both must be brought together! Religion and psychology are not adversarial; how can they be when we are fashioned by God? Rather than excluding either the emotional or the spiritual-doctrinal, we need to integrate them. God is to come to every plane of our thought and heart. It is such integration that both groups in the discussion were seeking.

Without efforts towards integration, opposite attitudes can creep in and then dominate. Those who hold to higher religious truths exclusively can come to reject psychological studies as unnecessary and corrupting, as a turning away from God. But to ignore or diminish the psychological feeling level is to not receive God fully. On the other hand, those who see the genuine value of psychology can look upon religious truths as pious theories, with no real application to the heart and emotions. Eventually religion can be seen as a banality. Yet this rejects God. Rather than such opposition, the two fields cry out for more and more integration. That is why this book has been written: as a step towards integrating the two beautiful fields of study and healing.

My hope also is to be of some help to the broken-hearted, spiritually and emotionally. There are so many who are in desperation or terrible anxiety. It is the nature of a loving God to heal, spiritually and emotionally. My hope and prayer is to be one of the servants of God in this healing.

Abbreviations

Abbreviations of the theological Writings of Swedenborg used in this volume:

AC	Arcana Caelestia
AE	Apocalypse Explained
AR	Apocalypse Revealed
CL	Conjugial Love
DLDW	The Divine Love and the Divine Wisdom
DLW	Divine Love and Wisdom
DP	Divine Providence
HH	Heaven and Hell
PTW	Posthumous Theological Works
SD	Spiritual Diary
TCR	True Christian Religion

All number references in the text refer to paragraphs, not pages, in conformity with Swedenborg's own numbering system.

All references to the Writings are from the Swedenborg Foundation (New York) standard editions, except for those from *Arcana Caelestia* Volume I (AC 1-1113) and *The Divine Love and the Divine Wisdom*, which are from The Swedenborg Society (London) editions (please see footnotes when these two are first referenced).

Part I

****
Mental Health
****

Chapter 1

Introduction: Which Self?

And the Lord God formed man of the dust of the ground, and breathed into his nostrils the breath of life; and man became a living being. The Lord God planted a garden eastward in Eden, and there He put the man whom He had formed (Gen. 2:7-8).

Many mental health professionals stress the importance of loving oneself, and their books reflect this: *The Psychology of Self-Esteem, Looking Out for Number One, Pulling Your Own Strings, The Self, Honoring the Self, Compassion and Self-Hate,* and *The Divided Self.*[1] Erik Erikson's *Identity and the Life Cycle*[2] is an early example. The philosopher Nietzsche and the novelist Ayn Rand approach the idea in different ways. One theme is that a good self image is the foundation of happiness. As Dr. Leo Buscaglia puts it: "To love others you must love yourself."[3]

What does this psychological trend mean to those searching for spiritual growth? How does it relate to 'loving your neighbor as yourself'? Can we love ourselves first without becoming narcissistic and selfish?

The underlying question is: how do we define 'self'? What gives us a separate sense of identity? The book *Conjugial Love,* written through Emanuel Swedenborg, states that "everyone has his own love, or a love distinct from another's love . . . . The reason why his love remains with every man[4] after death is because . . . love is man's life, and hence is the man himself."[5] So, the essence of our 'self' is what we love.

However, we love in many different ways in our lives. The theological Writings given through Emanuel Swedenborg often explain how different characters in Biblical stories symbolize different aspects within one person. We have many levels within us and we change so much during our lives. Our sense of ourself can be radically altered by adolescence, falling in love, mental illness, a brush with death, and other profound experiences. We pass through many selves or loves throughout our lives. At one time we may love innocence, at another time hatred. Even on the physical level, our cells die and are reproduced many times over.

Exploring the Writings, we can arrive at several distinct 'selves' or identities which can be experienced in the course of a lifetime. These are woven together in unity[6] but are based on different loves. These identities include the Divine endowment, hereditary love of self, remains (good childhood affections), the distorted self of mental illness, freedom of choice, the intermediate self, the subordinated love of self, and the heavenly proprium.

Which self are we to love? If we love ourselves too unconditionally we can overlook dangerous faults or evils. However, being overly self-critical destroys our peace and usefulness. We can find the balance by discovering which self we are *eternally* happiest identifying with—which self the Lord would bless us with. What are our qualities? What are the selves given us? What choice, or choices, give peace and joy?

Divine Endowment

I will praise You, for I am fearfully and wonderfully made;
Marvelous are Your works,
And that my soul knows very well...
Your eyes saw my substance, being yet unformed.
And in Your book they all were written,
The days were fashioned for me
When as yet there were none of them (Psalm 139:14-16).

Since, then, man by creation is a heaven in the least form, and consequently an image of the Lord, and since heaven consists of as many affections as there are angels, and each affection in its form is a man, it follows that it is the continual aim of the Divine providence that man may become a heaven in form and consequently an image of the Lord .... But its inmost is that man may be in this or that place in heaven, or in this or that place in the Divine heavenly man; for thus is he in the Lord .... Everyone who permits himself to be led to heaven is prepared for his own place in heaven ... and this is done by means of such an affection for good and truth as corresponds with it (DP 67-68).

We are created with our "own place in heaven" and we are led there if we allow it. Our "place in the Divine heavenly man" is formed by our spiritual work or use—the function we perform for the whole. For instance, angels of the mouth of the Grand Man initiate new spirits, as food is introduced before being assimilated into the whole body. There are an indefinite number of possible uses or functions. By the unique identity we are given, even before birth, we naturally incline towards performing our own special role. In heaven, each angel is thought of as the use he or she performs.[7]

The Divine endowment[8] defines one's inmost nature; one's life unfolds from it. It is one's inmost soul:

> In every angel and also in every man there is an inmost or highest degree . . . into which the Divine of the Lord primarily . . . flows . . . . This inmost or highest degree may be called the entrance of the Lord to the angel or man, and His veriest dwelling-place in them. It is by virtue of this inmost or highest that a man is a man, and is distinguished from irrational animals, for these do not have it. From this it is that man, unlike the animals, is capable . . . of being raised up by the Lord to Himself, of believing in the Lord, of being moved by love to the Lord . . . and of receiving intelligence and wisdom, and speaking from reason. Also, it is by virtue of this that he lives to eternity. But what is arranged and provided by the Lord in this inmost does not distinctly flow into the perception of any angel, because it is above his thoughts and transcends his wisdom (HH 39).[9]

Being Divinely endowed does not mean that we are merely robots. We have freedom of choice. Our inmost soul is analogous to our genetic structure, which forms and reforms our body throughout our lives. Identical twins can have nearly the same genetic structure and still look and act differently; we make our own choices within the limits of what we inherit physically. The Divine endowment forms our inner nature, but we make thousands of small choices along the way that help to shape us. We can also reject a heavenly endowment for use and turn to its opposite, because we are free.

We are given an affection for doing the use that forms our place in heaven. If we turn to the Lord, we love certain truths and goods that harmonize with our nature. For example, we may love to see how forms correspond to affections. While we are on earth this can manifest itself in the desire to be an artist, or an architect, or a flower arranger. After death we ascend discrete degrees and enter the inner use itself. Our 'place' in heaven is our primary state of spiritual love. There we are where we most love to be, we are who we most love to be, and we do what we most love to do. No wonder angels are "free indeed!"[10]

Hereditary Love of Self

And the Lord God commanded the man, saying, "Of every tree of the garden you may freely eat; but of the tree of the knowledge of good and evil you shall not eat, for in the day that you eat of it you shall surely die" (Genesis 2:16-17).

The worldly and bodily-minded man says at heart, Unless I am taught about faith and about things that belong to faith by means of sensory evidence so that I see for myself, that is, by facts so that I understand for myself, I am not going to believe. And he confirms himself in this attitude from the consideration that natural phenomena cannot be at variance with spiritual. Consequently it is from sensory evidence that he wishes to learn about heavenly and Divine matters. But this is no more possible than for a camel to pass through the eye of a needle. The more he wants by this method to become wise, the more he blinds himself, until in the end he believes nothing, not even in the existence of anything spiritual or in eternal life. . . . This is eating from the tree of the knowledge of good and evil. And the more he eats of it, the more dead he becomes (AC 128).

To eat of the tree of the knowledge of good and evil is to accept our natural or lower selves as gods or to believe "that there is no God, but that nature is what is called God, and that [we are] composed of the elements thereof."[11] Those who eat of the tree live by what is felt and sensed, and reason upward from this to spiritual things without opening up to heavenly influx. They also:

love themselves and the world above all things, . . . hatch out canons for the church from their own intelligence, and afterwards confirm them by the Word, . . . teach truths from the Word and live wickedly . . . [or] deny the Divinity of the Lord and the holiness of the Word (AC 128).

The term "Word" as used here refers to the great portion of the Bible that has a Divinely inspired, continuous symbolic meaning.[12]

We appear to live from ourselves and not from God. However, the Lord gives us our lives and that appearance so that we feel independently alive and are in freedom. "Man's premise must be from the Lord, and not self; the former is life, while the latter is death."[13] We must be willing to think "from the Lord" in order to grasp spiritual truths. Thinking from the 'serpent' of the senses alone is what caused the downfall of humanity's original innocence.

In a subtle form of spiritual genetics, tendencies of mind are passed from one generation to another. Selfish or selfless feelings that are consciously confirmed become etched within and are inherited as tendencies. This has been occurring since history began. Within each of us are tendencies towards hatred, cruelty and every other ugly quality we see reflected in the worst of what is around us in the world. Evil is not something imagined by 'pious' priests; it is the most cruel and destructive force in our lives. It is the killer of all that is innocent. However, the selfishness we inherit does not become attached to us unless we choose to confirm it. And it is powerful to realize that our spiritual choices affect people generations from now! We are all interconnected and woven into the whole.

The danger of believing solely in our innate goodness is that we have inherited tendencies to evil.[14] We also have the gift of good childhood affections. Neither is really our own; we are carefully balanced between them in freedom. Subtle spirits tried to lead Swedenborg to believe that people are basically good because their innermost minds are good. "But it was answered them that these inward and innermost minds were not theirs, but the Lord's . . . ."[15]

A part of ourselves must die before we can be reborn—the love of self which eats of the tree of the knowledge of good and evil:

> By the tree of the knowledge of good and evil is signified the man who believes that he lives of himself, and not from God; thus, that love and wisdom, charity and faith, that is, good and truth, are in man, his own, and not of God, believing this, because he thinks and wills, speaks and acts in all similitude and appearance as if from himself (CL 135).

The death of this false self-love is not an easy thing on the human heart; there is powerful agony in its removal. Honestly facing this reality, and shunning evil self-love with free inner discipline, is essential to rebirth. Evil and its pain are real, and must be faced and shunned before the Lord can lead us to be angels. The first chapter of *The Road Less Travelled*[16] by M. Scott Peck emphasizes this attitude toward the reality of spiritual and emotional pain as a key to real happiness and growth. And so does the whole Word of God.

Remains

The wolf also shall dwell with the lamb,
The leopard shall lie down with the young goat,
The calf and the young lion and the fatling together;
And a little child shall lead them (Isaiah 11:6).

Our first sense of ourself is basically the innocence and peace of infancy. This gives us a wonderful beginning to life, a paradise that we slowly grow away from. In childhood we are given the gift of feeling some of the thrilling aliveness of the angels. Deep in our memories is that sense of ourselves as trusting, loving and receptive. Such memories come from good loves in infancy and childhood that remain forever, if we protect them— and thus in the Writings are called "remains."

These remains give us a promise of what we can return to. In infancy, the 'power of ultimates' is at its height because we are so sensitive. Hidden within us are these potent memories of being loved and touched. They give us a vivid impression, on this plane, of what it is to feel the Lord's love. Deep inside we know what it is to be totally willing to be led by God.

8

We can use these powerful memories to help guide us, in an intuitive, feeling way, back to a sense of wholeness. We can become reconnected with heavenly influx and regain the vivid, enchanting outlook of childhood combined with the wisdom of a lifetime of spiritual growth. The means to do this are revealed in the Word: "I am the way, and the truth, and the life."[17] Truth honestly lived leads to good loves. And these good loves also remain, and are a part of us from the Lord. For remains are implanted all through our lives, though with a special power in childhood.

Distorted Self

> Lord, have mercy on my son, for he is a lunatic and suffers severely; for he often falls into the fire and often into the water (Matthew 17:15).

If we suffer from emotional disorders, we can become unbalanced and fall into the fire of self-hate; or we can feel a distorted love of self—a flaring self-pride and defensiveness. Hostility, a sense of personal superiority and narcissism can lead in extreme cases to murder or the illusion of being a king. Sick self-love or self-hate must be seen for what it is.

It is said in the Word of the insane man of Gadara: "neither could any man tame him."[18] Spiritually, a "man" represents or symbolizes truth. There is a type of distorted self-love in mental illness beyond taming by any obvious revealed truth. Like Narcissus, this love adores itself, and in this intense self-concern there is a sensitivity to put-downs or lack of attention by others. It is, in fact, ready to flare up in paranoia, imagining rejection where none exists.

What causes distorted self-love? Lack of love takes away all life;[19] so if love is not received through others in infancy, maybe it can come from one's self: intense and imbalanced self-love. Would not this distorted self-love be paranoic or self-protective, having already learned about rejection at the hand of others? A child desperate for love also however desires to please, and in this depends somewhat on distorted self-love for strength and leadership. The desire to please and the distorted self-love make strange partners.

What spirits are behind these strong stances? If they come during infancy or early childhood, they must be from influences of a powerful nature, since children receive direct influxes from higher and lower spiritual levels than adults. Distorted self-love must have strong spirits from hell behind it—one of those hells delighting in intense self-love—who welcome a temporary home in a wounded heart. So too with the desire to please—these conscience monger spirits have a powerful 'spirit' origin, especially since they ally themselves with the genuine innocence of childhood.

With less severe emotional disorders, those which are not completely crippling, normal loves operate, both good and evil. The 'normal' hereditary evil love of dominating would take distorted self-love to itself. What an alliance—two arrogant loves urging dreams of prestige, honor and wealth upon a susceptible psyche! It would take powerful help to confront these negative forces. That help will be there when the time is ready, as the Lord crossed the sea of Galilee to Decapolis in order to free the insane man of Gadara. The Lord can 'tame' the legion, and He will if invited. When necessary He will use natural means of healing the mind along with spiritual—for all healing comes from Him[20] even when a human agent (such as a psychiatrist) is involved.

Abnormal self-love and an excessive desire to please are pathetic; they are a cover-up for the pain of rejection—of no love. But the Lord's love can replace the emotional vacuum with loves, such as the conjugial, or true marriage love, in which He is directly present. Unrecognized rejection is like cancer, fostering the abnormal growth of false self-love. But if only the pain can be faced directly, then the Lord comes right to the state. Distorted self-love is removed. A new presence, the Lord and his inmost heaven, become a father and mother. The legion has been cast into the swine and into the sea.

This is where the plea for self-love or self-esteem so stressed in the psychological field has real validity. We need to discover the kind of love of self that is sound so that we may love uses and love others. A balanced, compassionate self-love is a key element in mental health and finally in spiritual health. The call for this kind of self-esteem is right! It is a necessity for true spiritual functioning. Unless we have a healthy, subordinated love of self, we cannot openly feel the higher loves of the Lord and the neighbor.

Yet 'Which self?' is still a pertinent question here. The sound love of self is sadly injured in mental illness. As compassionate self-love is restored, we feel a wonderful release. Remains that have been blocked off can inflow. It is a resurrection, with a deep sweetness, bringing a valid, fulfilling joy. We can enjoy loving ourselves because we never really have before. Then we can move on to the higher, happier state of loving others.

Freedom of Choice

The Lord God planted a garden eastward in Eden, and there He put the man whom He had formed. And out of the ground the Lord God made every tree grow that is pleasant to the sight and good for food (Genesis 2:8-9).

... The two trees, the one of "life," and the other of the "knowledge of good and evil," being placed in the garden of Eden, signified that freedom of choice in spiritual things was given to man.... Without such freedom of choice man would not be man, but only a figure and effigy; for his thought would be without reflection, consequently without judgment, and thus in the Divine things which are of the church, he would have no more power of turning himself than a door without a hinge, or, with a hinge, fastened with a steel bolt; and his will would be without decision, consequently no more active with respect to justice or injustice than the stone upon a tomb under which lies a dead body .... Man's life after death, together with the immortality of his soul, is owing to the gift of that freedom of choice.... Freedom of choice in spiritual things is from this, that man walks and lives his life in the midst between heaven and hell; and that heaven operates in him from above, but hell from beneath; and that the option is given to a man of turning himself either to higher things or to lower things... (*Coronis* 28).

We take in information from our senses and also experience thoughts, feelings and perceptions; then we decide what to do with it all. The deciding part is our freedom of choice or free will. It is the center that enables us to will this or that action. Our freedom of choice expresses our basic sense of ourselves as individuals.

"So long as man lives in the world, he is kept midway between heaven and hell, and is there in spiritual equilibrium, which is freedom of choice."[21] Our whole life on earth is a preparation for eternal life; the main task here is to choose where we want to be spiritually. We are in freedom from the Lord to love as we please and to settle into whatever level of spiritual growth we want, under His providence. It is this free choice that gives us a separate identity from God; and He wishes us to feel exactly as if this identity were our own![22]

Intermediate Self

A bruised reed He will not break, and smoking flax He will not quench, and He will bring forth truth into judgment (Isaiah 42:3).

This treats of the Lord; and "a bruised reed He will not break" signifies that He will not hurt sensual Divine truth with the simple and with children; "smoking flax He will not quench" signifies that He will not destroy the Divine truth that is beginning to live from a very little good of love with the simple and with children, "flax" signifying truth, and "smoking" signifying its being alive from some little love; and because both, that is, the "reed and flax" signify truth, it is said that the Lord "will bring forth truth into judgment," which means that He will bring forth with them intelligence, "judgment" signifying intelligence (AE 627:7).

Little children are basically in a state of innocence. However, anyone who spends enough time with them realizes that they have other qualities as well. We cannot become truly good until we go through the process of rebirth. The 'apparent goods' in childhood[23] have a selfish quality within them, but a child's innocence and ignorance make this appropriate:

... The goods of infancy ... although they appear good, are not good so long as hereditary evil contaminates them ....
Whatever is of the love of self and of the love of the world

then appears as good, but is not good; but still it is to be called good so long as it is in an infant or a child who does not yet know what is truly good. The ignorance excuses, and the innocence makes it appear as good (AC 1667:2).

When we are adults, good and selfish qualities combine in us like 'wheat and poisonous tares' until we become regenerate enough to "gather together the tares and bind them in bundles to burn them, but gather the wheat into my barn."[24] Until we allow the Lord to put away our selfishness, we are in this mingled state of 'mediate good.'[25]

> If anyone loves himself more than others, and from this love studies to excel others in moral and civic life, in memory-knowledges and doctrinal things, and to be exalted to dignities and wealth in pre-eminence to others, and yet acknowledges and adores God, performs kind offices to his neighbor from the heart, and does what is just and fair from conscience, the evil of this love of self is one with which good and truth can be mingled; for it is an evil that is man's own, and that is born hereditarily, and to take it away from him suddenly would be to extinguish the fire of his first life. But the man who loves himself above others, and from this love despises others in comparison with himself, and hates those who do not honor and as it were adore him, and therefore feels a consequent delight of hatred in revenge and cruelty, the evil of such a love as this is one with which good and truth cannot be mingled, for they are contraries (AC 3993:9).

Mediate good is necessary in rebirth. Because of the sheer force of hereditary selfishness within us, the 'fire' of our life requires love of self. Children feel an innocent self-merit when they get a gold star for their efforts. Ambitious young adults feel pride in their accomplishments. Feelings of merit are necessary stepping stones, filled with idealism. They spur us on until we reach a level of humility that doesn't need to be externally rewarded.[26]

There comes a time when we have to let the 'intermediate self' go in order to be truly happy:

> Such spirits as have confirmed themselves during their life in the world in the belief that the good they do and the truth

they believe is from themselves, or is appropriated to them as their own (which is the belief of all who place merit in good actions and claim righteousness to themselves) are not received into heaven. Angels avoid them. They look upon them as stupid and as thieves; as stupid because they continually have themselves in view and not the Divine; and as thieves because they steal from the Lord what is His (HH 10).

Subordinated Love of Self

And what does the Lord require of you
But to do justly,
To love mercy,
And to walk humbly with your God? (Micah 6:8)

There are three universal loves—the love of heaven, the love of the world, and the love of self.... Charity has something in common with each of these three loves because viewed in itself charity is the love of uses...the love of heaven looking to spiritual uses, the love of the world to natural uses, which may be called civil, and the love of self to corporeal uses, which may also be called domestic uses that have regard to oneself and one's own (TCR 394).

These three loves reside in every man from creation, and therefore from birth, and when rightly subordinated they perfect him.... These three loves are rightly subordinated when the love of heaven forms the head, the love of the world the breast and abdomen, and the love of self the feet and their soles (TCR 395).

While in mediate good, we tend to feel "that all love begins from self; that self is to be taken care of first and then others."[27] We know that we should 'love your neighbor as yourself,' but tend to stress the 'as yourself' part. Psychologically, 'looking out for number one' means: love yourself first and then you can love others. This is valid as a *temporary* attitude; but as we grow spiritually, it is turned around.

Man has been so created that he can look upward, or above himself; and can also look downward, or below himself. To look above himself is to look to the neighbor, to his country, to the church, to heaven, especially to the Lord; but to look

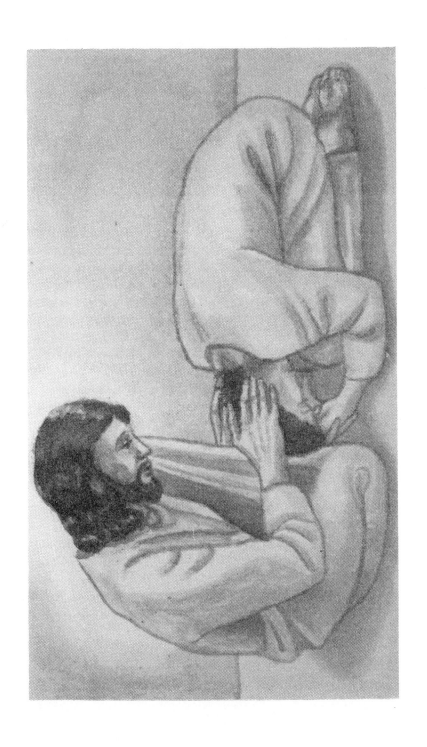

below himself is to look to the earth, to the world, and *especially to himself*.... To look above one's self is to be uplifted by the Lord; for no one can look above himself unless he is uplifted by Him Who is above.... Man looks below himself when he turns the influx of truth and good from the Lord to himself (AC 7814-7; italics added).

The man who is in the good of charity and faith *loves also himself* and the world, but not otherwise than as the *means* to an end are loved. The love of self with him looks to love to the Lord, for *he loves himself as a means to the end that he may serve the Lord* (AC 7818-9; italics added).

Loving ourselves comes beneath loving God and others. If we get to the point of looking up to the Lord first, taking care of others and then ourselves follows from an overflowing of love. We come to a state of trust that "takes no thought for the morrow." If we are feeling in harmony with all that is good around us and are performing useful services, our worry for ourselves falls away like a dead shell. Manasseh, Joseph's first-born son, represents this state: a 'forgetfulness' of self-interest.[28]

The story of the prodigal son illustrates the humility of genuine self-love. He left home with his inheritance and spent it all on 'riotous living.' He had to work feeding swine and still starved because of a famine. Then "he came to himself" and remembered his generous father. He decided to go home "and say to him, 'Father, I have sinned against heaven, and before you, and I am no longer worthy to be called your son. Make me like one of your hired servants.' "[29]

But his father was so happy to see him that he arranged a feast and gave his son beautiful clothes to wear: "for this my son was dead and is alive again; he was lost and is found." When, from the Lord, we find genuine humility and come to our 'true selves,' we are rewarded with a feast of love! Yet being humble does not mean being humiliated. It is full of the riches of spiritual life, coming from a genuine, open humility before the Lord:

When a man has been regenerated, consequently, when he has as the end to love the neighbor and to love the Lord, he then has as means the loving of himself and the world. When man is of this character, then when he looks to the Lord he accounts himself as nothing ... and if he regards himself as anything, it is that he may be able to serve the Lord (AC 8995:4).

To love our neighbor as ourselves we have to look to God, where that love begins. Before we begin regeneration, we naturally think of ourselves first.[30] Rebirth can open up a new sense of ourselves, realizing that we are not the center of the universe. Paradoxically, this realization brings us to far greater happiness and a higher sort of self-love.

Heavenly Proprium

And he showed me a pure river of water of life, clear as crystal, proceeding from the throne of God and of the Lamb. In the middle of its street, and on either side of the river, was the tree of life, which bore twelve fruits, each tree yielding its fruit every month. And the leaves of the tree were for the healing of the nations (Revelation 22:1,2).

"And he showed me a pure river of water of life, clear as crystal, proceeding from the throne of God and of the Lamb," signifies the *Apocalypse* now opened and explained as to its spiritual sense, where Divine truths in abundance are revealed by the Lord .... By "in the middle of its street, and on either side of the river, was the tree of life, which bore twelve fruits" is signified that in the inmosts of the truths of doctrine and of life in the New Church is the Lord in His Divine love, from Whom all the goods which a man does apparently as of himself, flow forth .... "Each tree yielding its fruit every month," signifies that the Lord produces good with man according to every state of truth with him .... "And the leaves of the tree were for the healing of the nations," signifies rational truths therefrom, by which they who are in evils and thence in falsities are led to think soundly, and to live becomingly (AR 932-936).

"To him who overcomes I will give to eat from the tree of life, which is in the midst of the Paradise of God."[31] If we invite the Lord into our lives, He helps us to overcome our hereditary selfishness and to become reborn into a new self. Remains give us the power to choose to subordinate our will to the Lord's. " 'I will give to eat from the tree of life' signifies or symbolizes appropriation of the good of love and charity from the Lord."[32] When we receive God's loving qualities and take them as our own, we become 'created in His image.'

The Latin word 'proprium,'[33] used in the Writings, has no English equivalent; it is what we appropriate to ourselves, what we take as our own. The proprium is a receiving vessel. The heavens flow into us through remains and our choices of good, the hells through hereditary evil tendencies and our choices of evil. We are born neither good nor evil. What we freely choose to make a part of ourselves forms our proprium, and this may be either good or evil.

God is life itself. When we choose to receive Him, we eat the fruits of the tree of life and become transformed—our proprium is made heavenly. The closer we come to the Lord, the more we realize that our very life is His in us:

> It is conjunction with the Lord that makes a man seem to himself to be free and therefore his own; and the nearer the conjunction with the Lord is, the more free he seems, and thus the more his own . . . because the Divine love is such that it wills its own to be another's (DP 43).

> The more distinctly a man appears to himself to be as if he were his own, the more clearly he recognizes that he is the Lord's, because the more nearly he is conjoined with the Lord the wiser he becomes . . . (DP 44).

A paradox of life and of religion is the revealed truth that all life is from the Lord, and yet we feel completely independent and that life is our own. There is a phrase in the Writings that speaks directly to this paradox: 'as of self' or 'as if of self.' This has two basic implications:

Firstly, the Lord wants us to feel life as of ourself. He wants us to feel exactly as though we are independently alive, apart from any outside source of life. Why? Because it is the very nature of Divine love to wish to give to others and to make them independently happy.[34] This is the 'of self' in the phrase.

Secondly, the Lord wants us to acknowledge that this independent life is an appearance, given by Him. Actually, He alone is alive; He is Life itself. All human beings are only receptacles of His life. This He 'shares' in the 'as of self' or 'as if of self' He gives to each of us.[35] The 'as' or 'as if' speaks of the appearance.

Thus the term 'as of self' cuts the Gordian knot of religion and life: we feel life convincingly as our own, but actually this very feeling is the Lord's gift! The paradox and thing of beauty is that the more we ascribe our life to the Lord in genuine honesty, the more independently alive we feel. The highest angels do this and so come into the heavenly proprium itself. This is how they discover the tree of life.

> The more clearly a man is conjoined with the Lord, the more distinctly does he seem to himself to be his own, and the more clearly does he recognize that he is the Lord's (DP 43).

> Abide in Me, and I in you. As the branch cannot bear fruit of itself, unless it abides in the vine, neither can you, unless you abide in Me. I am the vine, you are the branches. He who abides in Me, and I in Him, bears much fruit; for without Me you can do nothing (John 15:4,5).

Real freedom comes when we let go of the petty 'selves' within who hold us back. Free of self-centeredness and pride, we come into the endless bounty of the heaven the Lord can create within us. We are given spiritual life instead of a selfish life of our own. The difference becomes very apparent after death:

> ... When the things of man's [selfish] proprium are presented to view in the world of spirits, they appear so deformed that it is impossible to depict anything more ugly, ... so that he to whom the things of the proprium are visibly exhibited is struck with horror, and desires to flee from himself as from a devil. But truly the things of man's proprium that have been vivified by the Lord appear beautiful and lovely; ... and indeed, those who have been endowed with charity, or vivified by it, appear like boys and girls with most beautiful countenances; and those who are innocence, like naked infants, variously adorned with garlands of flowers encircling their bosoms and diadems upon their heads, living and sporting in a diamond-like aura and having a perception of happiness from the very inmost (AC 154).

Who Am I?

And out of the ground the Lord God made every tree grow that is pleasant to the sight and good for food. The tree of life was also in the midst of the garden, and the tree of the knowledge of good and evil (Genesis 2:9).

The 'self' is like every 'simple' thing—the closer you look at it the more complicated it becomes. A single cell is a universe in itself. The word 'I' seems basic but we contain many levels, some above our consciousness and powers of comprehension. How to 'love yourself' in a good way is no simple matter!

Who is the 'self'? From our inmost souls, we are formed 'in the image' of the Creator:

> That the Divine Love which is Life Itself and which is the Lord is in the form of the forms of all uses, which form is man, can be nowhere better seen than in the creation of the universe and then of the earth and of all things in them both. For, by creation there is nothing on the earth that is not made for use. The whole mineral kingdom is full of uses; there is not a particle of dust in it, nor any piece of soil formed of such particles, that is not of use. The whole vegetable kingdom is full of uses; there is not an animal, from the little worm to the lion, that is not of use and that is not also the form of its use.... In a word, every point in the created universe and in created beings is a use; in fact, it is a successively expanding series of uses from the use in first things to the use in ultimates, thus from one use to another in unbroken succession—clear proof that the Creator and Former, who is the Lord, is the infinite enfolding of all uses, in His essence Love, and in His form Man in whom that enfolding is (DLDW 20).

We are formed for a use; each of us is an integral part of creation. What we do affects the whole, not only now, but from now on. We can fulfill our Divine endowment to the highest possible potential, or fulfill it partially, or deny it. How we love ourselves shapes where we fit into the greater scheme of things. Do we subordinate self or does self try to subordinate all? Do we find peace in use towards others, or lack of peace in focusing too much on *self*-happiness?

The way we love ourselves decides which self we love. We can focus on the outer self we sense and feel and center our lives on it, or we can gradually turn towards the higher self within. By looking upward we take on a lifetime of spiritual challenge and increasing happiness, growing out of a narrow definition of who we are into a freedom that embraces the wonders of our eternal souls. We can feel so intensely alive that no words can touch the joy! And all this is a gift of the Lord our God.

Chapter 2

The Goal and the Setting

The Lord's Goal For Us

In the beginning God created the heavens and the earth
(Gen. 1:1).

"The beginning"...embodies within it that first period
when a person is being regenerated, for at that time he is born
anew and receiving life. Regeneration itself therefore is
called a new creation of man. "Heaven" means the internal
man, and "earth" the external man.[1]

According to the Writings given through Emanuel Swedenborg, the Word contains a consistent inner, symbolic meaning.
This 'internal sense' unfolds levels of truth to guide us on the
path toward rebirth into spiritual life. The first verse of Genesis
speaks of God's creating the universe; symbolically, it tells of
His creating a new person within each of us. Everyone has a
heaven and an earth within—inner and outer levels of the mind
waiting to be brought to life by the Lord. If we respond, He will
create in us an angel—a new person—a true heaven and earth
within. This is what Jesus meant when He said: "for indeed, the
kingdom of God is within you" (Luke 17:21).

The Lord's goal for us is that each of us becomes an angel. For
His very nature is Divine Love itself: the desire to love others
and give them eternal happiness. He would give us the gift of
heavenly life, a heavenly proprium. Thus we would, by rebirth,
come into our true self, our true identity, and discover what it is
to be fulfilled—eternally happy and useful.

But in the present we are usually far from this goal. As to our
lower selves, we are at times painfully aware that what the Lord
said of men of early times is still true: "then the Lord saw that
the wickedness of man was great in the earth, and that every
intent of the thoughts of his heart was only evil continually"

(Gen. 6:5). Of course there are times of sensitivity and uplifting, when we are carried up on wings of hope. But at other times we are appalled at our own coarseness. And throughout our lifetimes, with our different selves, our different and changing identities, how can the Lord's goal for us ever be accomplished?

It seems so easy, even simplistic, to speak of a heavenly self. Anxieties, disillusion, complete selfish orientation—these things often plague us. The body itself, with its appetites, often seems to betray us. We yearn to be better, but wonder how. Part of us may believe, but another is cynical. It is as with the man in Scripture whose son was possessed: "Lord, I believe; help my unbelief" (Mark 9:24).

Within certain identities in our hearts, there are giants in the land. Powerful forces are there, which oppose our ever becoming an angel. If a distorted self from emotional illness is present in any degree, it opposes any true change in spirit and heart. If our hereditary love of self is strongly operative, heaven is felt simply to be an illusion. These are giants of the spirit—enemy agents of which we are afraid. How can the Lord ever save us?

We can be saved because the Lord of creation is love itself, and His goal is heaven for us. He gives us our spiritual freedom, but other sweet gifts as well, to make angelhood possible despite inner giants. He gifts us with innocence in infancy. By means of this and many other secret means, He would lead us through our lifetimes on earth to another innocence: the innocence of wisdom in old age.

> Innocence is a receptacle of all things of heaven . . . it is a willingness to be led by the Lord, and not by oneself . . . . Children are led from the external innocence in which they are at the beginning, and which is called the innocence of childhood, to internal innocence, which is the innocence of wisdom. This innocence is the end (or goal) that directs all their instruction and progress; and therefore when they have attained to the innocence of wisdom, the innocence of childhood, which in the meanwhile has served them as a plane, is joined to them (HH 341).

> Assuredly, I say unto you, unless you are converted and become as little children, you will by no means enter the kingdom of heaven (Matt. 18:3).

Although it may not seem so, there is no force more powerful than innocence. This is because innocence is a trust in the Lord, a complete willingness to be led by Him. And He, the Lord God, is the most powerful force in all creation. When we are first conceived, He forms our soul with a Divine endowment for a heavenly use: a gift of future creativity that is sparkling with life itself. When we are born, He adds to this gift of our souls the sweet innocence of infancy. This is the start of a golden thread of human life, coming at the first moment of our birth. This golden thread is continued in its gentle leading throughout our entire lifetimes on earth. It leads from the innocence of infancy through our many changing identities as we grow and mature, to the innocence of wisdom in old age. And because it is the Lord who leads in this way, the golden thread is one that giants cannot break. If we choose to follow the Lord's Word, nothing in us or that attacks us can break this spiraling wonder. Temporary failures do not really harm it. What is said in the 23rd Psalm is eternally true: "The Lord is my Shepherd, I shall not want."

To see how the Lord leads us to heaven, to perceive the beauty and reality of this from the Word, we need His unfolding explanations and guidance. As much as we can, we will look then in this Book to the Lord's principles and explanations. He treats of each identity or self we experience throughout our life, describing the purpose of each. He would lead us by the hand, to see as much as possible of His purposes in the golden thread of human progress.

In the first chapter, we treated fairly briefly each of the identities or feelings of self the Lord gives us. Now, chapter by chapter, we would go into each of these identities in some detail. We would try to discover the Lord's purposes for us. Certainly He in His love and wisdom would have us become aware of some of the mysteries and beauties of the golden thread. And what is beautiful about this is that this investigation is not into abstract doctrine or difficult theories. There are of course profound things in creation that set the scene for the Lord to be with us; such things as the cosmology of creation and the structure of the human mind. But these things only set the scene for the most tender things in human life: infancy, motherhood

THE GOLDEN THREAD

SPIRITUAL AND MENTAL HEALTH

PART 1 — CREATION
- THE SETTING

PART 2 — THE LORD'S GIFTS
- SOUL, INNOCENCE, CELESTIAL LOVE

ENVIRONMENTAL ROLE (PARENTS, ETC.)

IMPEDE | FOSTER

PART 3

EMOTIONAL ILLNESS

BLOCKAGES
A) EMOTIONAL
B) METABOLIC

4

SPIRITUAL HEALTH

THE IDEAL:

CHILDHOOD
ABRAM/ABRAHAM

YOUNG ADULT
ISHMAEL/ISAAC

MIDDLE AGE
JACOB/ISRAEL

OLD AGE
JOSEPH

REORDER

EMOTIONAL HEALTH

HEALING
A) PSYCHOLOGICAL
B) SPIRITUAL

and fatherhood, discovering living faith, falling in love and finding true marriage love, and finding a job or use in which there is creativity and inner life. Even, in the end, discovering that we do not need to be afraid of death.

The Setting

"We know what we are, but know not what we may be."[2] That is we know our present moods and thoughts—when we feel open and content, when depressed or anguished. But what we "may be" is something else. We dream, we hope—but we know very little. God would have us know more. Within the Word is the overall design of the universe—heavens and earth—fashioned by God. Why did He create the earth? It is a place where we human beings choose our eternal destiny in the heavens or their opposites. The goal intended for each of us by God the Creator is the first thing He fashioned: the heavens. Here He would have us reside forever in the happiness and joy of being a useful person—an angel. But to have this choice be real and meaningful, He places us first upon earth, where we decide through our own free decisions what we become.

The Lord's first purpose is a "heaven from the human race."[3] His very nature is Divine love itself—love of others outside of Himself, to whom He wishes to give eternal happiness. Jesus said to His disciples: "This is My commandment, that you love one another as I have loved you."[4] It is this love, with its wisdom, that leads to the creation of human beings; that leads to the creation of the spiritual and natural worlds as dwelling places where we may live to discover the reality of the Lord's love. This love can change our lives and lead us to the discovery of heaven in our hearts, and can lead us to heaven as a dwelling place after the death of our earthly bodies:

> In my Father's house are many mansions, if it were not so, I would have told you. I go to prepare a place for you. And if I go to prepare a place for you, I will come again, and receive you to Myself; that where I am, there you may be also (John 14:2, 3).

To know something of the nature of human life and its true goals, there is a deep need to turn to the source of information:

God. What is His nature; what is He like? John the apostle saw Him on the Isle of Patmos:

> I was in the Spirit on the Lord's day, and I heard behind me a loud voice, as of a trumpet, saying: "I am Alpha and Omega, the First and the Last .... Then I turned to see .... And in the midst of the seven lampstands One like the Son of Man, clothed with a garment down to the feet and girded about the chest with a golden band. His head and His hair were white like wool, as white as snow, and His eyes were as a flame of fire. And His countenance was like the sun shining in its strength (Revelation 1:10-16).

This is a vision of the Alpha and Omega, the creator and Lord making Himself visible to human sight and comprehension. He is one, and His eyes are filled with the fire of gentle, infinite love. He calls us to Him, to a "mansion" or eternal home in heaven. "I am He who lives, and was dead, and behold, I am alive forevermore."[5] "I am the resurrection and the life."[6]

What is the overall picture or cosmology of creation? Where are the "many mansions" of the spiritual world, and what is this world like? First there is the Lord God Jesus Christ, the Alpha and Omega, who is the Creator. In fashioning creation, He started with a spiritual sun, the very first of finite creation.[7] The essence of this sun is His Divine love and wisdom, its fire being love and its light His wisdom:

> Although the sun of the world is not seen in heaven, nor anything from that sun, there is nevertheless a sun there, and light and heat, and all things that are in the world, with innumerable others, but not from a like origin; since the things in heaven are spiritual, and those in the world are natural. The sun in heaven is the Lord; the light there is the Divine truth, and the heat the Divine good that go forth from the Lord as a sun. From this origin are all things that spring forth and are seen in the heavens (HH 117).

> How great the Divine love is and what it is can be seen by comparison with the sun of the world, that the Divine Love is most ardent, if you will believe it, much more ardent than that sun. For this reason the Lord as a sun does not flow without mediums into the heavens, but the ardor of His love is gradually tempered on the way. These temperings appear as radiant belts around the sun; furthermore, the angels are

veiled with a thin adapting cloud to prevent their being harmed by the influx (HH 120).

What leads to the formation, the creation of each new human being? The Lord, in His wisdom, sees a new need in heaven to be filled. It is this, through human parental means, that leads to the creation of new souls: to conception, gestation and birth. A need in heaven leads to the fashioning of a new human being on earth. He or she is born as a tiny baby, but the Lord foresees in that infant a potential future angel—one who will, in freedom, meet the need seen in heaven by Him.

Above the highest heaven and below the spiritual sun there is a special dwelling 'place' of souls. This is on the plane of something like radiant belts,[8] the first degrees of the Lord's creation beneath the spiritual sun. This heaven of souls is also called the "heaven of human internals,"[9] for our souls are both human and the most internal thing within us. Upon this soul is placed a Divine endowment, a genius or gift for a certain heavenly 'use'—a totally fulfilling and creative service to perform for others. Every person born has such a beautiful endowment, a use from God. Each of us then is precious in His sight, in His love.

Below the 'radiant belts' are the three levels of heaven. The celestial plane is the highest, where the most innocent and loving angels live, those whose first love and thought are for the Lord. The second plane is the spiritual, where angels dwell who especially love truth and serving the neighbor. In the lowest level of heaven, the natural, live angels whose primary love is to obey. Every angel is part of a *society* of like-minded spirits, all working together as cells work together to form and sustain a human organ or other part of the body. These societies work in harmony with others, as organs function together to form a whole body. From His infinite vantage point, the Lord sees heaven as a *Grand Man*, with every angel performing a vital use to the whole.

'Below' heaven is the *world of spirits*, where those newly arrived from earth or the natural plane prepare for the transition to their spiritual homes. The inner loves that rule their lives surface, and extraneous emotions, pretenses and problems are sifted away or made quiescent.

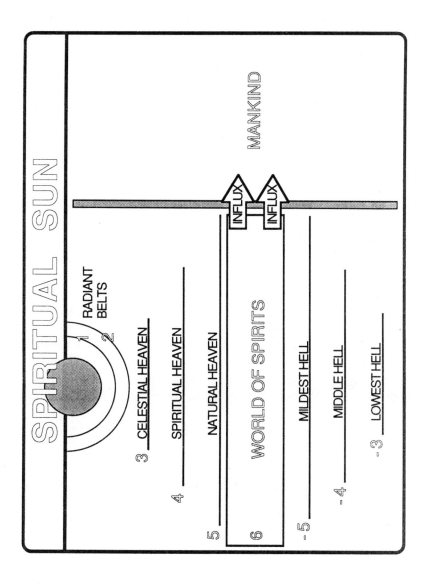

To leave us in total freedom, the Lord allowed for hells, which are ordered as opposites to the heavens. Thus, the lowest hell is a total perversion of the highest heaven. Every angelic society has its opposite—evil spirits who have a twisted version of that heavenly society's greatest love.

By creating all these realms for our spirits, the Lord gives us the freedom to become truly human—to be made in His image. Here on earth we can begin to become conscious of "what we may be." In the creation of new souls with a Divine endowment for use, the Lord gives new life—aliveness for a future use. In its inmost core, this endowment is creative love looking to serve; that is its very soul! The creation of each human being is as the hand of God, reaching out to touch Adam's hand, giving the gift of eternal life. And for each of us there is a *need*, a use, in heaven itself! And the goal in life is to achieve from the Lord our heavenly 'self' or heavenly proprium—for this self loves our use.

To become creative and useful angels, we need to become creative and useful people on earth. This means becoming healthy on every plane of ourselves—becoming whole in body, mind and spirit. Before our spiritual lives can flourish, our natural bodies and minds must be sound enough to provide a firm foundation. In this book we will explore early development and emotional growth, including emotional disorders and mental illness. From that basis, we will go through the stages of spiritual growth, culminating in the total freedom that comes with celestial love of the Lord. This love is the golden thread that weaves through our lives, touching us at every vital step when it is needed.

It is this golden thread that leads us throughout our lives from our conception to our future homes in heaven. Guided by the Lord we start with a Divine endowment, and from birth are gifted with remains or heavenly affections. The Lord leads us through infancy, childhood and youth towards adult age, and its gift of free choice. Then, as adults, we can begin to follow the golden thread to a higher and higher identity or self—until the Lord gifts us with a heavenly proprium. It is this unfolding of life on earth, from infancy to the final promises of regeneration, that is the subject of this book.

Chapter 3
"And He Blessed Them"

And the Spirit of God was hovering over the face of the waters (Genesis 1:2).

"The Spirit of God" is used to mean the Lord's mercy, which is said "to hover," like a hen over eggs, over what the Lord stores away in man and which in the Word are frequently called *remnants* [or "remains"]. These remnants are cognitions of truth and good which never come to light or into daylight until external things have been laid waste. These cognitions are here called "the face of the waters" (AC 19).

Each person's inheritance is unique, imprinted on the structure of the first cell that divides after conception. This uniqueness is also written on the inmost soul, because each soul is formed with a purpose to fulfill. Everyone is created to perform for the whole of creation as the cell performs for the whole body. The Writings say that heaven functions as a *Grand Man*, with each angel playing a part in its life.

Of each human being it may be said of the very beginning of life in the womb:

...I am fearfully and wonderfully made;
Marvelous are Your works,
And that my soul knows very well.
My frame was not hidden from You,
When I was made in secret,
And skillfully wrought in the lowest parts of the earth (Psalm 139: 13-15).

The Lord conjoins Himself to man in the mother's womb as soon as conception takes place, and forms him.... While man is in the womb, he is in a state of innocence; his first state after birth, therefore, is a state of innocence; and it is only in man's innocence that the Lord dwells with him.... Man is then in a state of peace likewise.[1]

The embryo has no life of its own, but has the Lord's life within.[2] It is alive, but is not conscious of it, protected in the heart of the Grand Man. Special celestial angels surround the unborn baby, angels who are in "heavenly joy more than others."[3] The independent life of the individual comes with the first breath.

Birth

Behold, children are a heritage from the Lord,
And the fruit of the womb is His reward (Psalm 127:3).

Conscious life begins when the lungs, which correspond to the understanding, are opened at birth.[4] The newborn infant is touched on the inmost level with feelings of innocence and peace. These surrounded him unconsciously in the womb, but now they are *experienced* on a beautiful, inner level.

This carryover of peace and innocence from the womb is not always seen at birth and immediately after. However, *Birth Without Violence* by Frederick Leboyer[5] shows a way in which birth can carry a sense of exhilaration and innocence. Through the intelligent, compassionate use of touch, the infant can be brought from peace in the womb into peace at birth.

The peace and innocence of the first celestial impressions with the newly born are impossible to define easily. They have within them a deep trust, an utter looking to the Lord as the sunshine of life, and an innocent willingness to be led by Him. These loves, or inmost impressions, remain as the deepest human feelings. In the Writings they are termed 'remains'; or remnants, because they can remain forever.

The very first state after birth is outwardly obscure,[6] a corporeal or bodily state. This is the almost helpless, dependent infant of the first days and weeks. Externally, the baby is animal-like;[7] but within, on the highest or celestial level, this is the most tender state of life. The inmost peace and innocence are with the baby even though above his or her outer consciousness.

Nothing in creation can harm this first state.[8] Even within the worst forms of mental illness, a secret level remains untouched. This sanctuary provides a balm and a connection with love and wholeness, a first trust that is inviolable. It is implanted no matter what the external circumstances are; and if it cannot be given, the baby dies.

> Few, if any, know how man is brought to true wisdom. Intelligence is not wisdom, but leads to wisdom; for to understand what is true and good is not to be true and good, but to be wise is to be so. Wisdom is predicated only of the life—that the man is such. A man is introduced to wisdom or to life by means of knowing (*scire et nosse*), that is, by means of knowledges (*scientias et cognitiones*). In every man there are two parts, the will and the understanding; the will is the primary part, the understanding is the secondary one. Man's life after death is according to his will part, not according to his intellectual part. The will is being formed in man by the Lord from infancy to childhood, which is effected by means of the parents, nurses, and the little children of a like age; and by means of many other things that man knows nothing of, and which are celestial. Unless these celestial things were first insinuated into a man while an infant and a child, he could by no means become a man (AC 1555:2).

The origin of this first trust is from the Lord through the soul and the celestial heaven. As mentioned before, in the cosmology of the Writings, the inmost soul is on the plane of something like radiant belts which immediately surround the spiritual sun. These are the first and second degrees of the Divine 'proceeding' (or flowing into creation). The celestial heaven is on the third level. The spiritual heaven is on the fourth level, the natural heaven on the fifth, and we on earth are on the sixth.[9] Each level is distinctly above the one below it, immensely more powerful.[10]

Imagine the power of the influx in infancy, coming from three discrete levels above earthly life! The baby is surrounded by the highest angels, who are in a celestial love of the Lord. Many of these angels lived on earth during the golden age of the Most Ancient Church, in the infancy of the human race. They live incomparably more fully than we do. All of their senses are extremely acute; their perceptions, affections and thoughts are above our ability to imagine!

According to Leboyer, newborns are incredibly sensitive. Their hearing is finely tuned, their eyes hurt in light, and their skin is very tender. He guesses that they "feel a thousand times more intensely than we do."[11] It would make sense that babies are enveloped in the sphere of the most innocent and sensitive angels. We can feel some of this peace surrounding an infant.

The celestial remains of little children are of three degrees:

> When first born, man is introduced into a state of innocence, in order that this may be a plane for all the succeeding states, and be the inmost of them; which state is signified in the Word by "suckling." Next, he is introduced into a state of the affection of celestial good, that is, of love toward his parents, which with such infants is in the place of love to the Lord; and this state is signified by an "infant." Afterwards, he is introduced into a state of ... mutual love, that is, of charity towards his playmates, which state is signified by "boys" [also little children] .... Innocence is immediately from the very Divine, and thus is the very essential in them all (AC 3183:1,3).

What is the celestial? It originates in loving others more than oneself, and this is the key to its nature as felt by infants and small children. Their love of their parents stems from celestial love.[12] It is ideal that children feel that their parents love them this fully, more than themselves. For from this feeling and perception infants know what heaven is.[13]

Touch

> Then they brought young children to Him, that He might touch them; but the disciples rebuked those who brought them. But when Jesus saw it, He was greatly displeased and said to them, "Let the little children come to Me, and do not forbid them; for of such is the kingdom of God" .... And He took them up in His arms, put His hands on them, and blessed them (Mark 10:13-16).

Loving touch is the means through which the Lord instills highest celestial remains. Since infants are in a sensuous state externally,[14] the inflowing celestial love is received by the senses, especially the sense of touch. Through touch babies feel love and thus celestial good.

Parents are in place of the Lord in infancy. Their hands on

And He Blessed Them

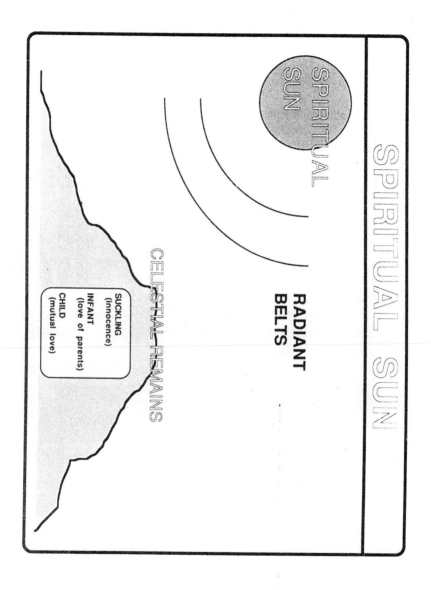

36

the baby are a powerful living symbol of what the Lord did: "He took them up in His arms, put His hands on them, and blessed them" (Mark 10:16). Actually, what parents do for their children is done truly on behalf of the Lord; and in the other world the Lord becomes the parent. Parents are the first symbols of the Lord—and more than symbols: they serve for Him in this world, in the giving of love, protection and nourishment.[15] The sense of touch is vital in this role:

> The sphere of innocence flows in also into the souls of parents, and conjoins itself with the same sphere [of innocence] with the infants, and ... is insinuated especially by the touch .... That the communication and thence the conjunction of innocence takes place especially through the touch is manifestly perceived from the pleasantness of carrying them in the arms, from embracing and kissing them, above all with mothers, who are delighted with pressing the mouth and face against their bosoms, and then at the same time by the touch of their palms there ... and also from stroking their ... body .... Communications of love and its delights between married partners are made through the sense of touch .... Communications of the mind are also thereby effected, because the hands are the ultimates of man and his primary things are together in the ultimates. By this sense, moreover, all things of the body and all things of the mind that are intermediate are held together in unbroken connection. Hence it is that Jesus touched infants (CL 396).

Parents expressing their love for a child with touch is vital for infants. Psychological studies show that the lack of such loving expression causes severe emotional problems. "The Divine in heaven which makes heaven is love .... Everyone who reflects can know that the inmost vitality of man is from love, since he grows warm from the presence of love and cold from its absence, and when deprived of it he dies."[16] Studies have shown that some babies in orphanages died for want of loving touch. In less severe cases, unloved infants raise up defenses that undermine emotional health.

The sense of touch is very powerful, and should be used gently and steadfastly, but not demandingly or obsessively.

Leboyer has much to say about this in *Birth Without Violence*.[17]
The Writings describe a wrong use of touch:

> With natural [selfish] fathers and mothers, the love of infants
> is indeed also from innocence, but this, received by them, is
> wrapped about their own [ego-centered] love, and hence they
> love infants from the latter and at the same time from the
> former, kissing, embracing, carrying, taking them to their
> bosom, and fondling them beyond all measure . . . (CL 405).

To hold and touch with love is not to possess, but to give!

A mother holding and caressing her infant with love is a
means used by the Lord to convey the most profound celestial
remains. Such remains are the foundation for all spiritual
growth. Touching evidence of this is seen in Swedenborg's
experience in the spiritual world: "I have seen infants and
mothers in light of so great a brightness and resplendence that
there could not possibly be anything brighter" (AC 1523). The
Lord Himself as an infant showed the way:

The order was that the Lord should first of all be

> imbued from infancy with celestial things of love. The celes-
> tial things of love are love from Jehovah and love to the
> neighbour, and innocence itself in these. From these, as the
> veriest fountains of life, flow all other things both in general
> and particular, for all other things are merely derivations.
> These celestial things are insinuated into man chiefly in his
> state of infancy up to childhood, and in fact without knowl-
> edges; for they flow in from the Lord, and affect him, before
> the man knows what love is and what affection is; as may be
> seen from the state of infants, and afterwards from the state of
> early childhood (AC 1450).

Innocence

Out of the mouths of babes and infants
You have ordained strength (Psalm 8:2).

Within our earliest states, the Lord creates a golden thread
that giants cannot break. Affections are implanted that protect
us throughout life. These celestial states overcome even the
lowest hell and enable us, from the Lord's power, to win victory
in adult spiritual temptations. Remains allow us to be reborn.
". . . And a little child shall lead them."[18]

Innocence never dominates, yet it is the strongest force in creation. It is from the Lord as the Lamb and has all power. As John the Baptist said when he saw Jesus: "Behold the Lamb of God, Who takes away the sin of the world."[19] All evil is fought from innocence, for "the removal of evils, and the implantation of good and truth . . . are effected through the good of innocence by the Lord."[20]

The supreme symbol of the power of innocence is the birth of the baby Lord in Bethlehem of Judea: "and she brought forth her firstborn Son, and wrapped Him in swaddling cloths, and laid Him in a manger."[21] "For there is born to you this day in the city of David a Savior, who is Christ the Lord. And this will be the sign to you: You will find a Babe wrapped in swaddling cloths, lying in a manger."[22]

Innocence is within every other love, including conjugial (marriage) love and love of the Lord; it makes us truly human. Therefore, it is the first gift of the Lord to us, instilled in earliest infancy, though long since forgotten by our conscious minds. ". . . It is only in man's innocence that the Lord dwells with him."[23] It is here, perhaps incredibly to our adult minds, that the Lord has come nearest to us in our lives. "The Lord is . . . much more present with little children than with adults."[24]

Inmost remains are reawakened in extreme crises or temptations, and then the Lord is again present. He is also most present with those who reach the celestial degree of rebirth—who come into the innocence of wisdom. But these, too, are children—wise children, who have followed the golden thread from the innocence of infancy to the innocence of wisdom, and the two have been conjoined by the Lord. "In a word, the wiser the angels are the more innocent they are, and the more innocent they are the more they appear to themselves as little children. This is why in the Word 'childhood' signifies innocence."[25]

This rebirth or regeneration is a far richer state of innocence and peace than what is experienced in infancy. It is a state of wisdom, of consciously receiving celestial love. Then the world again becomes as alive as it was in childhood, and "a happy and blessed feeling flows from the interior man into the delights of . . . [sensuous] things, and increases them a thousandfold."[26]

Chapter 4

Love of Children or Storgé

"Who is My mother and who are My brothers?" And He stretched out His hand toward His disciples and said, "Here are My mother and My brothers! For whoever does the will of My Father in heaven is My brother and sister and mother" (Matthew 12:48-50).

Although the word 'storgé' does not appear in most dictionaries, it is defined in the *Oxford Universal Dictionary* as: "natural affection; usually that of parents for their offspring."[1] The term is not unique to the Writings, but they have enriched its meaning. Two types of storgé exist: spiritual, looking to the eternal welfare of children; and natural, the more instinctual love held in common with animals. There is nothing wrong with natural storgé unless it becomes united with selfishness.

The story of King David and his son Absalom is a vivid example of the harm selfish natural storgé can bring. Absalom was handsome and a natural leader, but he was also treacherous. He deceived and misled many of the Israelites into joining him in a rebellion against his father. He was finally defeated in a battle that took his life. Even though his son had been determined to kill him, David's grief at Absalom's death was heart-wrenching:

> "Oh my son Absalom—my son, my son Absalom—if only I had died in your place! O Absalom my son, my son!...." So the victory that day was turned into mourning for all the people.... And the people stole back into the city that day, as people who are ashamed steal away when they flee in battle (2 Samuel 18:33, 19:2,3).

It is moving that David could mourn so much for Absalom in spite of the rebellion. However, David was ignoring the greater good—the people who had risked their lives to stand by him. He

40

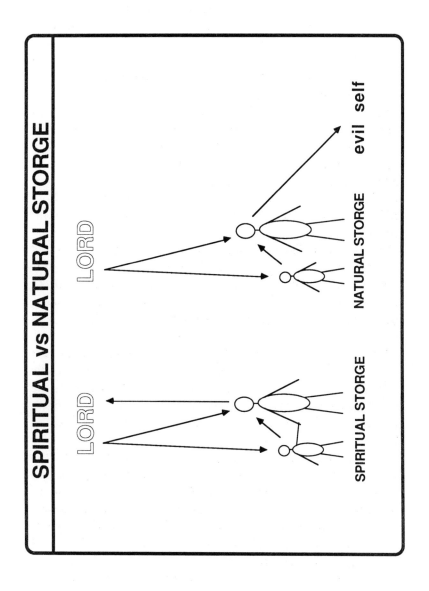

mourned so obsessively that his general, Joab, warned that he would lose the faithful people who had fought for him if he could not show appreciation. It was natural, selfish storgé—seen in his putting his son before his country—that obsessed King David.

The father of the prodigal son also loved his son deeply, but in this case he was willing to let go when the boy wanted to strike out on his own. The son wasted his inheritance on wild living and ended up working like a slave. Then he remembered his father and sincerely repented. He returned home where he was greeted with open arms: "for this my son was dead and is alive again; he was lost and is found."[2] This relationship was spiritually oriented because the father was detached yet still very loving. He was willing to let his son leave and return without bitterness over the boy's mistakes, and he felt inner joy over his son's repentance.

We see countless examples of both types of storgé in the world around us. Parents feel both at different times. Certainly it is easier to be spiritually inclined handling a fragile, innocent newborn than a rebellious adolescent. How can parents maintain a spiritual outlook towards their children? Where does storgé come from?

Storgé is one of the most powerful human emotions because it helps to fulfill the Lord's primary purpose—a heaven from the human race. Heaven, and its eternal happiness, are what the Lord wants to give us. To this end, children are born of conjugial love, and protected by storgé, so that they can discover eternal warmth and joy.

Storgé arises from Divine love flowing secretly into the inmost of parents' minds. Conjugial love and storgé go hand in hand, both coming first to the mother, who unconsciously transfers them to the father.[3] Love of children is first awakened by a stirring of innocence within the heart of the mother early in gestation, when the highest angels are guarding the potential new angel. They awaken innocence in the heart of the mother that will respond overwhelmingly to the innocence of her newborn child.[4]

Innocence, which is the willingness to be led by the Lord,[5] is beautifully seen in Mary, the earthly mother of Jesus Christ.

"And Mary said, Behold the maidservant of the Lord! Let it be to me according to your word."[6] The inspired words of Mary to her cousin Elisabeth show genuine storgé:

> My soul magnifies the Lord, and my spirit has rejoiced in God my Savior. For He has regarded the lowly state of His maidservant; for behold, henceforth all generations will call me blessed. For He who is mighty has done great things for me, and holy is His name (Luke 1:46-49).

After a child is born, the mother's innocence joins with the baby's innocence. Then storgé, which has its soul from innocence, is fully and consciously experienced. Parents need to receive innocence in their souls and minds, or else "they would be affected in vain by the innocence of infants. . . . Otherwise, it would be like a tender seed falling upon flint, or as a lamb thrown to a wolf."[7] They then choose how to act about this feeling:

> To appearance, the love of infants with spiritual married partners is similar to the love of infants with natural married partners; but with the spiritual, storgé is more internal and thence more tender. . . . The spiritual love their children according to their spiritual intelligence and moral life; thus they love them according to their fear of God, or piety of life, and at the same time according to their affection for and application to uses serviceable to society, that is, according to the virtues and good morals with them.

> With natural fathers and mothers, the love of infants is indeed also from innocence, but this, received by them, is wrapped about their own love. . . . They love them, not on account of any fear of God and . . . piety of life, nor for any rational and moral intelligence in them, and little . . . do they consider their internal affections and thence virtues and good morals, but only things external for which they have regard (CL 405).

Seeds of Rebellion

What man is there among you who, if his son asks for bread, will give him a stone? (Matthew 7:10)

Naturally oriented parents attach their love to external things in their children, closing their eyes to faults. "The reason is that the love of their progeny is with them also the love of themselves; and this love clings to the subject outwardly, but does not enter into it."[8] In spite of powerful personal feelings, spiritually oriented parents look to the greater good, realizing that they do not do their children any favors by ignoring problems or incipient evils.

The real test is not what parents feel, but what they do about their feelings. Feeling selfish storgé is almost inevitable; the highest challenge is to steer away from it and consider the child's spiritual welfare. This is the greatest gift parents can give to their children, because it can last forever. When love is wisely guided in this way, the Lord can operate through parents to touch eternally the heart and mind of a child.

Children can be deeply hurt by the absence of spiritual storgé. Celestial, spiritual and moral loves are implanted successively from infancy to youth. These loves are from the Lord through angels, and are instilled simultaneously with the growing child's experiences. They are innocent loves of the Lord (celestial loves), of the Word (spiritual loves), and of idealism (moral loves). These powerful loves remain throughout life, and so are termed 'remains.' Parents are often a primary means of implanting them, through gentleness, patience and thoughtful attention. If their attitude is selfish, children won't find these loving qualities in them. Instead, children will see false demonstrativeness, or inattention, impatience and even careless cruelty.

Since they live in a garden of tender and fragile loves, children are extremely sensitive to such attitudes. Where there is parental rejection or false possessiveness, they suffer deeply. Spiritually, they lose most precious affections which should come directly through the father and mother. The Lord must work in other ways to instill remains.[9]

> Remains are preserved with every human being, so that a free choice of heaven is possible. But there can be more or fewer remains. Thus we read: "the fewer remains there are, the less he is a man, and the more remains there are, the more he is a man. Remains are like some heavenly star, which, the smaller it is the less light it gives, and the larger, the more light" (AC 530).

Selfish natural storgé is not content with an influx of innocence alone. It demands that the parental ego control in a possessive way. It wants rewards, not actually for the child, but for self. It is excessive, requiring that the parental ego be satisfied, without thought for the true good of the child. This is a non-human love which pretends to be very human, dominating over innocence and crushing or smothering instead of nurturing. This smothering of innocent and tender states in a child is deeply harmful in itself. But there is more, because when love is not implanted, its opposite inflows. Hatred will ensue when selfish storgé fails to supply heavenly love.

Selfish natural storgé betrays itself. Children can quickly sense the self-centered nature of love, either being lavished upon them for the wrong reasons or offered stintingly as a reward for 'good behavior.' They turn away or secretly withdraw with inner revulsion. In early years this may be unexpressed through shyness or fear, and because they hope for genuine love. But adolescents often express it with rebellion and burning contempt for their parents.

If parents strive for spiritual storgé—trying to be fair to all of their children, looking to spiritual qualities, then hatred can be largely kept out of the parent-child relationship. This is attained when patience, firmness, interest and thoughtful action are substituted for impatience, laxity, disinterest and false sentimentality. If parents recognize and shun selfish tendencies in themselves, the purity and genuine tenderness of the family relationship can be maintained. Highest remains can be instilled and protected, and the sweet innocence of storgé is not hurt by selfishness in parents.

Loving discipline comes from unselfish love of children. Children do not object to discipline if there is real love behind it; they respond to any evidence of genuine love. What they do mind is discipline that is simply love of dominion; raw striking out from anger reaps separation and the death of love. This happens within the heart of a child and will show itself later in adult life.

"Our Father, who Art in Heaven"

He who loves father or mother more than Me is not worthy of Me. And he who loves son or daughter more than Me is not worthy of Me (Matthew 10:37).

Parents and children are usually closest during the children's infancy. After that time:

> In the degree in which the innocence with infants recedes, affection also is remitted, and conjunction, and this successively even to separation. Storgé recedes from parents according to the recession of innocence with children . . . even to the [eventual] separation of the children from the home; and among beasts and birds even to the rejection of them from their presence, and forgetfulness that they are of their stock (CL 398).

Ideally children are seen as wonderful, temporary gifts from the Lord. Parents then raise them knowing the children are not really theirs, and are willing to let go, to grant independence to children-become-adults. Children are not possessions! But natural storgé never loses its possessiveness. Love of self cannot release; it must rule.

Parents are guides and mentors to their children; but with adulthood, children come into their own liberty and rationality. Then they guide themselves according to their own consciences, looking to the Lord instead of parents. With selfish storgé, there is a strong desire to hold on and rule, denying adult status to children. In contrast to this, spiritual storgé fosters a deep delight that children, on becoming adults, have accepted the Lord as their guide. Parents should be truly willing to let go of the previous relationship, and feel spiritual joy when their grown children turn to the Lord.

One difficulty in breaking the parent-child relationship when the children have become adults is that for years the liberty and rationality of the children were in their parents' hands. When children reach maturity, their own rationality and liberty are fledglings, while parents, being more experienced, could probably guide the new adults better than they can guide themselves. However, parents need to grant their children the same freedom the Lord gives to His adult children—the freedom to guide one's self, even though this leads to mistakes and errors. Freedom is nothing unless it includes freedom to err. Although parents may suffer deeply for their adult children, they should not interfere. They can give advice if the child, as a friend, asks for it. But if they interfere, the inner motive is not from heaven but from the love of dominion, because they are denying the basic qualities that make a human being: liberty, or free choice, and rationality. Enforced denial only leads to rebellion, bitterness and heartache.[10]

Yet family ties are not necessarily broken on earth or after death. One bond should be broken, the one that is forged by parental government and the resulting submission and dependence of the child. That rightly belongs only to the period of childhood. After that, only the ties of free affection remain.

Some of the most powerful heavenly remains are associated with parents. While we are on earth, all affections are associated to some extent with something in time and space. In infancy, the mother and father are the living symbols of the Lord to children. This association is not completely lost until after death, when we rise above things of person, time and space. Throughout our earthly life, we associate deepest remains, wonderful loves, with our parents, even though there is independence.

Parents too have deep spiritual remains or affections associated with their children, for the storgé they feel during their child's infancy is a stirring of genuine innocence. As long as they live on earth, they associate these deep-seated remains of innocence with their children. This loving bond holds a family together throughout life on earth. It encourages parents and adult children to have strong adult friendships—as equals!

After death, families meet again. Deep bonds of affection can hold them together at first, while they are relatively the same as they were on earth. But as they become more and more spiritually oriented, inmost remains are dissociated from things of time, space and person. Depths of innocence are separated from their attachment to persons, and innocence is felt as it is in itself. This may also happen on earth to some degree.

Association in the spiritual world is according to loves, and to loves alone, as with Jesus when He spoke of His mother and brothers: "For whoever does the will of My Father in heaven is My brother and sister and mother."[11] If we live with our families in heaven, it is because our spiritual loves are very similar; but the fundamental relationship is that of adult to adult. The earthly parent-child relationship is not only dissolved, it is actually forgotten. The relationship of angel to angel is much deeper and far more sensitive than any family relationship on earth, for the loves of angels are immeasurably deeper and closer than ours. They are truly 'at home,' surrounded by those who think and feel as they do. "A father of the fatherless ... is God in His holy habitation. God sets the solitary in families; He brings out those who are bound into prosperity...."[12]

Chapter 5

Emotional Disorders

And when He had come out of the boat, immediately there met Him out of the tombs a man with an unclean spirit, who had his dwelling among the tombs; and no one could bind him, not even with chains, because he had often been bound with shackles and chains. And the chains had been pulled apart by him, and the shackles broken in pieces; neither could anyone tame him. And always, night and day, he was in the mountains and in the tombs, crying and cutting himself with stones (Mark 5:2-5).

Inmost celestial remains provide a foundation for future spiritual growth. The Lord gives this base to everyone to maintain spiritual freedom. If remains cannot be sufficiently implanted, infants will die. Remains instill an inner core of warmth and light that balance the cold and darkness within hereditary evil and leave us in freedom to choose our own spiritual destiny. At times such remains give little outward appearance of being present, as in severe mental illness, but they are there, waiting to be effective, when blocks are removed.

Children are protected by remains and also by storgé, which every parent feels to some degree; it is "equally with the evil as with the good; likewise with gentle and ungentle beasts; yea, . . . with evil men and with ungentle beasts it is sometimes stronger and more ardent."[1] Still, we need not look far to see children and adults suffering from lack of love and some form of emotional disorder. Very few of us are totally free of any emotional disturbances. No matter how much the Lord subtly pulls to 'gather us under His wing,' He has left humanity in freedom—even to hurt itself.

Spiritual growth is directly affected by emotional disorders.[2] This growth can even be halted in mental illness, which is more severe than emotional disorders. Remains are still protected within, but open access to them is cut off. To be reborn, we must have freedom and rationality, qualities of a clear and whole mind. We need the freedom to make our own choices and we need to understand enough about life to make those choices. Spirituality can grow normally only when the emotional level is basically healthy and stable. If our minds become distorted by severe emotional problems or mental illness, the process of rebirth cannot unfold.[3] Spiritual growth is suspended until we are sufficiently healed, in this life or the next. This is why I will treat of mental health first in this book, and then go on to speak of spiritual wholeness.

Some New Church people feel that the Writings alone will give healing and answers to all problems—all sicknesses of mind or spirit. This very affirmative attitude has a real truth within it. All natural things do have spiritual causes, and spiritual causes are dealt with in the Writings. "He shall guide you into all truth."[4] The Writings give spiritual teachings to lead us towards rebirth. However, they do not give full treatments of natural or scientific truths. These are areas to study and develop in academic scholarship, in a way that both natural and spiritual worlds of truth may combine.[5] In fact, such combined studies are part of the genius of this planet, part of what it offers to the heavenly performance of uses.

The Writings do not prescribe natural medicines for physical diseases, nor do they speak much about that part of mental/emotional disorder that is on the natural plane.[6] They cannot be expected to since they focus on what is eternal. However, spiritual principles can shed light on the devastation that these disorders inflict on the human mind. The Writings do define their parameters, listing the emotional states and mental outlooks involved. And then they make the point that such mental illnesses are natural, not spiritual (DP 141).

What is happening in emotional and mental disorders? What are the causes, and why does the Lord permit such suffering? Since answers are not directly given in the Writings, they will come through professional (psychological) research and experience. Still, there are truths in the Writings which apply and are very helpful. Certainly, emotional disorders and mental illness call for as much study as physical illness; cures are desperately needed. We are still in the early stages of finding ways to heal the emotionally crippled.

In this book, I have deliberately used very few psychological terms—Freudian, Jungian or more recent ones. One reason for this is that the Writings use their own distinct terms, a number of which cover those used in psychology—especially areas of psychology that enter into the spiritual mind or into the basic nature of the mind as fashioned by the Lord. For instance, the 'spiritual world' and the 'human internal' embrace much of Jung's 'collective unconscious.' The 'hereditary love of self' is part of the 'id,' 'freedom of choice' and the 'subordinated love of self' are similar to the 'ego.' The 'superego' includes conscience, both true and false.[7] Where terms of the Writings and of psychology coincide to some degree, I prefer to use terms of revelation. Of course, there are many psychological terms that do not apply to what is in the Writings, since the two fields focus on different levels of the mind.

However, there is a growing interest in the interplay between the spiritual and natural levels. Some fields of psychology are exploring mental health issues in a way that is in harmony with religion. They are involved in holistic healing, studying the inter-relatedness of body, mind and spirit. Following in the footsteps of people like William James (who wrote The Varieties of Religious Experience and whose father was a student of Swedenborgian thought) and Carl Jung (who also read Swedenborg's works), they are opening up psychology to higher levels.

Jung said that he never had a cure that was not religious! When released from emotional illness, a person becomes spiritually free as well. What a wonderful, profound and powerful experience! Spiritual growth can finally proceed after one has been released from mental and emotional bonds.

Mind and Body

You have laid me in the lowest pit,
In darkness, in the depths...
You have put away my acquaintances far from me;
You have made me an abomination to them;
I am shut up, and I cannot get out (Psalm 88:6-8).

Mental and emotional blocks have a tremendous effect that often goes unrecognized. They bar remains from inflowing freely into the natural plane of the mind, keeping us from feeling the love that was there in infancy and leaving us feeling isolated and alienated from the love of those around us. The less this paralyzing barrier is recognized, the more powerful its grip can be.

In mental illness the emotions and conscience are crippled, disturbing the reception of healthy spiritual influx. Something in the natural plane of the mind distorts the reception of remains:

> No one is reformed in unhealthy mental states, because these take away rationality, and consequently the freedom to act in accordance with reason. For the mind may be sick and unsound; and while a sound mind is rational, a sick mind is not. Such unhealthy mental states are: melancholy, a spurious or false conscience, hallucinations of various kinds, the grief of mind from misfortunes, and anxieties and mental suffering from a vitiated condition of the body. These are sometimes regarded as temptations, but they are not. For genuine temptations have as their objects things spiritual, and in these the mind is wise; but these states have as their objects natural things, and in these the mind is unhealthy (DP 141).

This passage gives two causes of emotional/mental disorders: one, undefined, on the emotional/mental level of the natural mind, and the other on the same plane of the mind but caused by a "vitiated condition of the body."[8] This allows for two of the major causes of mental illness given by professionals in psychology: an unloving childhood environment, and biochemical or bodily influences. Swedenborg made it clear in a letter that "insanity reside[s] in the external natural man and not in the internal spiritual."[9] Although emotional disorders can affect spiritual growth, they are not on the spiritual level.

There can sometimes be spiritual growth while suffering from emotional disorders:

> Inasmuch as at this day few undergo spiritual temptations, and consequently it is not known how the case is with temptations, I may say something further on the subject. There

are spiritual temptations, and there are natural temptations. Spiritual temptations belong to the internal man, but natural ones to the external man. Spiritual temptations sometimes arise without natural temptations, sometimes with them. Natural temptations exist when a man suffers as to the body, as to honors, as to wealth, in a word, as to the natural life, as is the case in diseases, misfortunes, persecutions, punishments and the like. The anxieties which then arise are what are meant by "natural temptations...." But spiritual temptations belong to the internal man, and assault his spiritual life. In this case the anxieties are not on account of any loss of natural life, but on account of the loss of faith and charity, and consequently of salvation.... There is also a third kind [of temptation], namely, melancholy anxiety, the cause of which is for the most part to be found in an infirm state of the body or of the lower mind. In this anxiety there *may be something of spiritual temptations, or there may be nothing of it* (AC 8164; italics added).

This passage again gives two causes for emotional/mental disorders: 1) "an infirm state of the body" and 2) "an infirm state of the lower mind." Again, the origin of the infirm state of the lower mind is not explained. "Melancholy anxiety" (depression) may come entirely apart from spiritual temptations, or "there may be something of spiritual temptation." It seems that extreme cases of mental illness are on the natural plane of the mind *only*, and cut off spiritual growth.[10] However, milder emotional disorders can be endured *during* the process of rebirth. It may even become a part of the process since the Lord only allows evil if it can be turned towards good.

"Of the Lower Mind"

I am like a man who has no strength,
Adrift among the dead,
Like the slain who lie in the grave,
Whom You remember no more,
And who are cut off from Your hand (Psalm 88:4-5).

What are the elements in our natural minds that block the reception of remains? Parents are a medium of instilling remains through love. What if they fail to feel love toward a child or more likely fail to express it adequately and tangibly? What if the child finds it difficult to receive love? What is the effect? "He grows warm from the presence of love, and cold from its absence, and when deprived of it he dies."[11] If parents express love stintingly, children may not die, but something within them can "grow cold" or "die." What effect will this psychological death have on the mind?

'Quality' love by parents—love of an infant that is tender and perceptive—is the key factor in instilling inmost remains by the Lord. When a parent's love is obsessive or excessively pampering, the wrong love of self will be nourished in the infant. He or she will be 'spoiled,' a more limited receiver of unselfish and gentle affections.

In defining emotional/mental disorders, Swedenborg lists: "anxiety,"[12] "melancholy" and a "spurious or false conscience."[13] There can be many complex reasons for mental imbalance; parents are not necessarily the cause. In severe mental illness, some infants are mentally distorted at birth, ruling out a parental *cause* of lack of felt love after being born. Certain severe sicknesses, such as syphilitic insanity with a parent, can mentally distort an infant's natural mind from birth. Sometimes the very disposition of an infant seems out of harmony with that of the parent, and this can be a limiting factor in giving and receiving love. Still, the earliest years in the home are so powerful in shaping children's emotional lives. Could parental coldness produce many of these emotional problems in a child?

But the Lord is not limited to working through parents to instill remains! He is Divinely caring, and will use other environmental means to gift children with inmost states. There is that beautiful teaching of the *Arcana*:

> The will is being formed in man by the Lord from infancy to childhood, which is effected by means of the parents, nurses, and the little children of a like age; and by means of many other things that man knows nothing of, and which are celestial (AC 1555: 2).

Fear

I suffer Your terrors (Psalm 88:15).

Anxiety is a common denominator in emotional and mental disorders. There is a continual 'worry' quota, sometimes intense, sometimes less so. What is this anxiety really about? At its worst, its core is fear, even horror, with a sense of panic. If the deepest love of infancy—love of parents (and the Lord through them)—seems to be gone, how would children feel? The parent, often the mother, is the center of their love at this stage—their very life. If that love is withdrawn—or apparently absent— wouldn't anxiety, fear and panic flow in? When deprived of love, we "die." This extreme fear would block the influx of remains and spiritual growth:

> No one is reformed in a state of fear, because fear takes away freedom and reason, or liberty and rationality; for while love opens the interiors of the mind fear closes them; and when they are closed man thinks but little, and only of what then presents itself to the mind or the senses. Such is the effect of all fears that take possession of the mind (DP 139a).

This passage treats of adults, but fear with a child has a similar effect: it closes the way to the interiors of the mind. Remains then are unable to flow in gently and freely. Within this fear or anxiety, carefully covered over because of its potent effect, is a deep pain at the apparent absence of love. This hurt is a death-inviting force; to get rid of it, death is preferable. Death can be invited in a number of ways, some less obvious than others. Such moods, hidden even below consciousness, have the effect of intensifying the original anxiety.

Not all anxiety or fear stems from deprivation of love. Other factors also induce fears, such as the death of a loved one, being physically abused, and desertion. But a sense of loss of love could play a crucial role in each of these cases. There are also external or natural fears, by which the Lord governs evil states.[14]

Melancholy

My eye wastes away with grief,
Yes, my soul and my body!
For my life is spent with grief,
And my years with sighing (Psalm 31:9-10).

'Melancholy,' is no longer used as a technical term in the mental health professions; still, it is accurate. There is often a deep sadness in emotional disorders that is openly or obscurely tied in with death, such as a fear of death and sickness. Hope is tenuous, almost gone. Could this come from a death of love early in childhood? If the deep remains of love are blocked, children would grieve as "Rachel weeping for her children, and would not be comforted because they are not."[15]

I once went to visit a woman who was so depressed that she just gave up. She lay down to die; all she could see was darkness. She went through therapy and is better now. Her feelings were extreme, but black moods can overcome us so that it seems impossible to go on. We lose all our vitality and sense of humor. It feels as if we are in a deep hole and there is no escape.

False Conscience

And Jephthah made a vow to the Lord, and said, "If You will indeed deliver the people of Ammon into my hands, then it will be that whatever comes out of the doors of my house to meet me, when I return in peace from the people of Ammon, shall surely be the Lord's, and I will offer it up as a burnt offering." ... and the Lord delivered them into his hands .... When Jephthah came to his house at Mizpah, there was his daughter, coming out to meet him with timbrels and dancing; and she was his only child (Judges 11:30-34).

A spurious or false conscience led Jephthah to sacrifice his daughter. Within our concept of duty we may have certain false standards—false vows—that can harm our usefulness and endanger our only daughter, our higher affection. We tend to think of conscience only as something good, but there can be too much of a good thing. If conscience is overdone and out of balance, it can cause real problems.

We may think of our conscience as an inner dictate that will warn us when we are about to do wrong and automatically flood us with remorse if we give in to evil. We may imagine it as the angel on our right shoulder, telling us what is right and heavenly. The Writings warn that these concepts are false and dangerous. The conscience is simply the leading ideas we believe and love; we call these 'truth.' Often such 'truth' is partly false and can lead into internal agony. A true conscience is based on a balanced and enlightened understanding of the Lord's teachings. "In Your light we see light."[16]

A false conscience can develop early in childhood, when parental love is a child's very life. If there seems to be a danger of losing this love, children will do almost anything to win it back. They will strive to be perfect if necessary. Perfectionism is common in emotional disorders. False conscience drives people on to overwork, to do everything as perfectly as possible. A child may unconsciously feel that "if my parents don't love me, somehow I have failed them." So the child has to make up for it, must do things perfectly. Often in this syndrome there are rituals, repetitive patterns of habit, that are a part of being 'perfect.' But they don't really make sense. They are a symptom of the disorder—part of the desire to regain love—an almost fanatical need.

There are spirits surrounding us who complement our natures and affect thoughts and feelings. In the case of perfectionism, they can flow in with "conscientious scruples in unimportant matters:"[17]

> ...spirits...that raise scruples in matters where there need be none; because they burden the conscience, they are called conscience mongers. What true conscience is, they know not, because they make everything that comes up a matter of conscience: for when any scruple or doubt is suggested, if the mind is anxious and dwells on it, there are never wanting things to strengthen the doubt and make it burdensome (AC 5386).

The mind must be released from this mental trap before a true conscience can emerge. This means becoming aware of what is distorting the conscience and making it "burdensome." The direct remedies are in approaching the Lord in personal prayer, accompanied by the shunning of specific evils that we know are contrary to Divine order. Usually it will be one of these evils in particular that harasses us, and we need to shun it from the Lord's help and strength but still with our own initiative. An indirect remedy is talking to another person—a counselor or friend.[18]

The Word can help to clear up the false conscience, if it is studied prayerfully and with trust in the Lord. We will begin to see trifling things as trifles, petty rituals as such without inner spiritual meaning. The release comes gradually but surely. "I am the way, the truth, and the life."[19] The time may well come when truth, lived, becomes the heart of good within us from the Lord. And then from this wonderful good, insights of truth can come that are perceptions of genuine conscience. Such a conscience, the gift of the Lord, is free from the conscience mongers that may have plagued us. But the conscience is never perfect in its intuitions, even the celestial angels learn.[20]

Anger

I am distraught.
Your fierce wrath has gone over me;
Your terrors have cut me off.
They came around me all day long like water;
They engulfed me altogether.
Loved one and friend You have put far from me,
And my acquaintances into darkness (Psalm 88:15-18).

Depression is often the face of hatred and fear, an outer mask that depletes energy. Beneath it is a sense of defeat, a death of love, and also anger that can have a killing force. Absalom, King David's son, was handsome and regal, and the people adored him. But underneath the shining exterior, he was ruthless. He killed his brother, schemed against David, and overthrew him. Like the people, we can be fooled into thinking that anger is good, and nurture it. Really, it is a killer, in some cases literally.

Hatred is often suppressed in emotional or mental disorders; honest soul-searching may eventually reveal a burning anger.

58

At best it is zeal, at worst it is full of the venom of hate, with cruelties of many kinds. There may even be the secret desire to kill, and an unconscious, frightening joy in that feeling.

Love is the fire of life. Ideally, this is a good love; if not, it will be the fire of self-love or selfish love. Nature abhors a vacuum. The spirit is lifeless in a vacuum of loves.[21] *Some* love must be present for life: good, evil, or a mingling of both.[22]

If we are deprived of love as small children, we are going to be angry:

> ...Anger exists or is excited when any one or any thing is contrary to one's love, by which there is conjunction with any one or any thing. When this conjunction is broken, the man becomes angry or wrathful, as if something were lost from the delight of his life, and consequently from his life. This sadness is turned into grief, and the grief into anger (AC 5034).

We may secretly hate the parent who fails us. When we are so innocent, this hatred is unacceptable. It feels wrong, so the hatred is buried, or projected onto someone else. We may search frantically for the lost love in other people, in money, goals or objects, never facing the well of grief and anger within us. We may even transfer our need for love to religion, using it as a defense against facing our emotions. But this is not genuine religion.

It is even easier to set up a substitute person to be hated openly, instead of a parent who is also deeply loved. This projection is common, on both spiritual and emotional levels. It is so easy to see someone else's faults. The ones we particulary dislike bear a strange resemblance to our own shortcomings. Psychologically, it is more comfortable to blame someone besides the parent. From remains, we love our parents, who do have many good traits. So, authority figures are substituted—the boss, the policeman who stops our car, even our spouse—but not the parent. We may even project the anger onto our own children, perpetuating the vicious chain. There is a tendency to project inner torment to the outer environment. Such projections can lead to hatred of institutions or races, rather than seeing that the real problem, the real evil or trauma, is in one's own heart and mind.

An even better substitute, and especially good since it will hurt no one else, is ourselves. Better to hate ourselves than our parents! We may feel suicidal without knowing why. We want to kill what is hated in ourselves; that will solve the problem! One form of suicide is drug or alcohol abuse, which just takes more time. In one case when I was trying to persuade someone not to commit suicide, he said that what he was doing was innocent, for the sake of others. Maybe, in a twisted way, it was. Maybe it was remains seeing the terrible unrecognized anger and hate and saying 'I am not worthy to live. That hate is unacceptable.'

This is not to say that discovering that a part of us that may hate our parents will magically cure everything. If this hatred is at the root of an emotional disorder, uncovering it is only the beginning. Awareness of the problem is the first step on the road to recovery; understanding and forgiveness can only come when the anger has surfaced and been faced honestly. Then the wound can begin to be healed.

Guilt

Though I have stolen nothing,
I still must restore it (Psalm 69:4).

Anger towards parents is very painful to early innocence. Innocence has already been deeply scarred in emotional disorders and mental illness by lack of love. That a child also has to bear hatred towards a parent seems like too great a burden. Perhaps this is an explanation for the huge sense of guilt often felt in these disorders. There is a feeling of failure, and a striving to make up for it, undermined by a sense of despair. This could be another factor behind spurious conscience. The innocence from remains is so powerful that if a child feels guilt, from remains grieving over his or her own hatred of a parent, it could devastate a whole lifetime.

In certain spiritual areas or emotional states, the intention has the force of the deed. The two are seen, or worse *felt*, as one. To hate one's parent can lead to the next emotional step: to kill the parent in the mind. This is done mostly without conscious recognition, and that unrecognized killing is a source of influx

of special hells which find their delight in hate and its fulfillment in killing. So, in their emotions, children may secretly
'kill' a parent who has failed to give them love or who has
mentally or physically abused them.

If prior to this killing an inmost love has been implanted for
that very parent, there is a dichotomy: love and hate trying to
coexist in the same mind. What greater cause could there be for
emotional illness? Also, what greater cause for a terrible burden
of guilt? This kind of guilt does not come from conscious
breaking of the Ten Commandments; it comes from a tender,
childlike mind trying to defend itself from trauma. Guilt is
probably one of the most potent factors in mental illness. Why it
is there, or even *that* it is there, has to be faced first. Then, with
help and courage, it can gradually be removed in the healing
process. If this cannot be accomplished completely on earth, it
will be in healing sanctuaries after death.[23]

Swedenborg tells of an incident that shows the effect that
parents can have on children:

> I was in the street of a large city and saw some small boys
> involved in a fight, . . . and I was told that the parents them-
> selves urged their children into these fights. The good spirits
> and angels who were seeing these events through my eyes
> were so repelled that I could feel their horror—particularly at
> the fact that the parents egged their children into such situa-
> tions. They said that parents in this way snuff out at this early
> age all mutual love that infants have from the Lord, and lead
> them into attitudes of hatred and vengefulness. As a result, by
> their deliberate behavior they deny their children access to
> heaven, where there is nothing but mutual love (HH 344).

Anger, fear and guilt are at the root of many emotional
problems. They are giants that frighten the innocent child
within. They are not like the hatred that we as full adults can
allow to become a part of us. If we are mentally ill, these evils are
not confirmed as our own; we are a victim of them. We may
have both righteous zeal and burning anger towards some
injustice in childhood coupled with a fear of losing love. Often
this is a fear of losing the parent we both love and hate. So, the
emotions are denied consciously and become unconscious

bogey men who haunt nightmares and cripple emotional growth.

Still, within us, the Lord is guarding and the angels are watching over the golden thread. No giants will be allowed to sunder that thread.

"Of the Body"

According to the Writings, there are physical as well as other causes of emotional/mental disorders. Melancholy or depression can come from an "infirm state of the body,"[24] and anxieties and mental suffering from a "vitiated condition of the body."[25] The physical component of mental health is now being widely studied.

There has been a change in approach towards the mind-body relationship in recent years. In traditional psychiatry, drugs are given which alleviate the symptoms of mental or emotional illness. They can be valuable in allowing people to function relatively normally so that they do not have to be institutionalized and can respond to therapy. Newer approaches are changing theories on the causes of mental illness, definitions and healing techniques. Some are focusing on physiological and biochemical causes, emphasizing new medicines and treatment, and/or nutrition. Nutritionally based treatments involve diet changes, vitamins, and other methods to restore chemical balance and improve overall health.

There are those who say that physical and nutritional factors are the only causes of emotional and mental disorders. The Writings also include an infirm state of the "lower mind" in distinction to the body.[26] Reflecting more deeply, the cause-and-effect relationship so prominent in the Writings might lead us to think that causes of emotional illness are primarily on the inner level of the natural mind, apart from an infirm state of the body. If there is warfare in the inner emotions, the battle would send out shock waves which would affect the body's chemistry. However, both physical and natural-mind disorders are listed as causes. Both factors are present, sometimes one taking priority as cause, sometimes the other.

If there are both physical and mental causes of emotional problems, then it makes sense that healing can be facilitated by a holistic approach that recognizes the interplay of spirit, mind and body:

> The internal man cannot live a spiritual life unless the external man is in agreement.... It is the same with the external sight relatively to the internal sight. If the external sight has been injured, it cannot any longer serve the internal sight; for if the external sight distorts objects, the internal cannot see by means of it except with distortion.... It is the same in the case of the natural or external man relatively to the internal man: if the memory-truths in the external or natural man are perverted or extinguished, the internal man cannot see truth, thus cannot think and perceive except pervertedly or falsely (AC 9061).

This distortion happens "when the external man has been injured."[27] Although these passages are speaking in terms of regeneration on a spiritual level, I believe the principle involved would apply to injuries on the natural plane of the mind. Drug or substance abuse would inflict such injuries. Emotional injuries also distort the clear perception and affection of the internal man, impeding or stopping regeneration in severe cases. In less severe illness, progress can be made in rebirth but with some blocking and distortion.[28]

Why?

> Where can I go from Your Spirit?
> Or where can I flee from Your presence?
> If I ascend into heaven, You are there;
> If I make my bed in hell, behold, You are there.
> If I take the wings of the morning,
> And dwell in the uttermost parts of the sea,
> Even there Your hand shall lead me,
> And Your right hand shall hold me (Psalm 139:7-10).

Why does the Lord permit emotional disorders and mental illness, since they involve so many states of anxiety and sadness? The universal principle is that "the permission of evil is for the sake of the end, namely salvation."[29] What seems overwhelming in the present may be a necessary and brief agony from the viewpoint of eternal salvation.

> Nothing can be permitted without a reason, and the reason can be found only in some law of the Divine providence, which law teaches why it is permitted (DP 234e).

> No one is reformed in unhealthy mental states, because these take away rationality, and consequently the freedom to act in accordance with reason (DP 141).

> The Lord permits evils of life that man may not fall into the most grievous kind of profanation (DP 233:13).

> The means of rebirth and the government of the Holy Spirit involve many things unknown to man (AC 4063).

The Lord would never permit suffering without a good reason. Since spiritual progress is not usually made in mental illness, such illness is probably permitted to protect inmost remains. Mental illness is better than any deep harm that has eternal consequences. However, that is only one possibility; secret goods are probably also done beyond our understanding. Certainly, out of emotional disorders and mental illness come lessons of compassion we might never discover any other way. The following passage refers to spiritual insanity (evil), but I believe it applies to the natural mind as well:

> There appeared a wonderful representation which continued for some time. The representation was to show how [spiritual] insanity variously combined is made subservient to the affecting of the mind with gentle and sweet sensations.... When ... I was still considering what could be made of those unhappy, and as it were insane souls in the other life, and of what use they could be to themselves and to others, ... I at length perceived that ... such delights could be effected as flow into innocent states and affect them in a wonderful manner, and indeed by Divine Omnipotence, that they may be arranged ... into so wonderful a connection of things, that delights may hence be produced, so as to affect happy minds, and especially infantile and innocent states. Thus insane states, even the most sad, and in the highest degree misera-

ble, are made subservient under the guidance of God . . . to the production of gladness and delight. Thus these delights are hence promoted as luxuriant crops of corn are produced from the dust of the ground. I was also permitted to experience a species of gladness from the angels of God Messiah—a gladness arising from the idea that such things as in themselves are unhappy and miserable are, nevertheless, made subservient to use . . . . (SD 231).

Chapter 6

Possession?

And always, night and day, he was in the mountains and in the tombs, crying out and cutting himself with stones. But when he saw Jesus from afar, he ran and worshipped Him. And he cried out with a loud voice and said, "What have I to do with You, Jesus, Son of the Most High God? I implore You by God that You do not torment me." For He said to him, "Come out of the man, unclean spirit!" Then He asked him, "What is your name?" And he answered, saying, "My name is Legion; for we are many" (Mark 5:5-9).

What effect do spirits and angels have on our lives? We do not normally have any perception that they are with us. The Lord wants us to feel that our lives, our loves and hates, are our own. Our lives are fed by what we love—what we choose to take in and make a part of ourselves. The Lord does not intend us to be consciously aware of the spirits who are with us. This leaves us in freedom to choose our own destiny—to be truly human and alive. However, we are alive from angels and spirits!

...For a man to have communication with the spiritual world there must be joined to him two spirits from hell and two angels from heaven, and without these he would have no life whatever. For a man cannot possibly live from general influx, as do animals void of reason; because his whole life is contrary to order; and being in this state, he would necessarily be acted on by the hells only, and not from the heavens; and if he were not acted on from the heavens he would have no interior life, thus no life of thought and will such as is proper to man, and not even such as is proper to a brute animal, because a man is born without any use of reason, and can be initiated into it solely through influx from the heavens (AC 5993:1).

Although we are unaware of it, the natural and spiritual planes are both within us. Our minds form a bridge between the two worlds. Beings from our spiritual 'family' are unconsciously with us all the time, affecting how we think and feel. We determine the quality of the spirits with us by the quality of our lives. Although they are with us, we are still left in freedom. This is essential to being human.

"My Name Is Legion"

Then one was brought to Him who was demon-possessed, blind and mute; and He healed him, so that the blind and mute man both spoke and saw (Matthew 12:22).

Can we be possessed by spirits, like the man from Gadara whom Jesus healed? While Jesus was on earth he closed off the hell of spirits who possess people bodily. There can no longer be that kind of external possession.[1] However, our minds can become possessed if we knowingly yield to malicious tendencies:

When [these wandering spirits] have entered into the taste with man, they possess his interiors; namely, the life of his thoughts and affections.... Very many at this day are possessed by these spirits; for there are at this day interior obsessions; but not, as formerly, exterior ones. Interior obsessions are effected by such spirits; and their quality may be evident if attention is paid to the thoughts and affections, especially to the interior intentions which they are afraid to manifest; and which are so insane with some, that unless they were restrained by external bonds ... they would rush into murders and rapine more than the obsessed ... (AC 4793).

This type of possession is not permitted by the Lord with those in unrecognized evils; it occurs only when in free choice we yield knowingly to base evils.

If we become emotionally or mentally imbalanced, we feel torn by emotions that assail us. We can be kept awake by anxious thoughts, preyed upon by bouts of depression, driven to irrational perfectionism, or besieged by a host of other problems. These feelings are not something we have chosen for ourselves knowingly. We feel caught in the trap of our own minds. With severe illness, we can feel driven to acts of violence, 'out of our minds' and 'out of control.'

The Gadarene was torn by a legion of demons. The Writings imply that there are a legion of spirits hidden within mental illness, struggling to dominate us. 'Conscience monger' spirits lead to the false conscience of obsessive perfectionism. Spirits full of hate want us to get revenge and even kill. Killer or 'death' spirits sway people towards unconsciousness with drugs, alcohol, or suicide ("cutting himself with stones"[2]). They persuade people to blame themselves when they should not. Anxious spirits intensify fear of a loss of love, and instill terror. Bodily symptoms accompany these emotions: tension, inability to sleep, trembling, psychosomatic pain, and so on.

Most people suffering from emotional or mental disorders are unaware of the influence of these troubling spirits. They feel life as their own and so are left in freedom. They feel anxieties or fears, but are unaware of the spirits inflowing into such moods. The spirits themselves want us to reject the idea of their existence; this gives them more subtle power. Psychologist Wilson Van Dusen describes startling confirmations of these spirit influences in *The Presence of Spirits in Madness*,[3] where he describes cases of extreme states of illness. The hallucinating patients with whom he worked heard and were affected by beings that fit the Writings' descriptions of angels and devils. This seems to be a breakdown of the normal wall between the worlds, a wall that is there for our protection. In milder emotional disorders there is no direct awareness of troubling spirits, only the fears and anxieties they bring. But in severe mental illness, the barrier can be broken and spirits do obsess.

Open Communication with Spirits

And he said, "No, father Abraham; but if one goes to them from the dead, they will repent." But [Abraham] said to him, "If they do not hear Moses and the prophets, neither will they be persuaded though one rise from the dead" (Luke 16:30-31).

As we go through our lives on earth, we are always in contact with angels and spirits unconsciously. In the normal progress of life we are rarely if ever aware of them. Using the Word as an objective guide and shield, we can apply the truth we learn to our lives, so that it can touch and shape our affections and emotions. Gradually our selfish tendencies can become humbled and put away so that we can be reborn. As this process occurs, we may be blessed at times with the Lord's or the angels' directly touching us, awakening us to spiritual realities not felt ordinarily. This can happen in times of great need, in states of deep worship or more frequently if we are regenerating. But it only happens unexpectedly and when it would not take away our freedom and compel belief; it is a beautiful experience that can confirm our faith.

Our first priority is to seek the kingdom of heaven. The Word is the Lord Himself talking to us; we don't need open communication with spirits when we have the Lord teaching us in revelation! It is important to seek a personal relationship with the Lord through prayer (which is "speech with God"[4]), but not to seek miracles and visions. If people on the path to rebirth "hear anything about a miracle [or contact with spirits] they give thought to it only as an argument of no great weight that confirms their faith; for they think from the Word, and thus from the Lord, and not from the miracle."[5]

The Writings warn against actively trying to contact spirits. The ones most eager to reach us are those who are dissatisfied with their lives, who want to 'borrow' our senses to live on earth again through us. Evil spirits openly communicating with us can pose as wise teachers, leading us away from our true path. They take malicious delight in this misdirection.

> ...At the present day to talk with spirits is rarely granted because it is dangerous; for then the spirits know, what otherwise they do not know, that they are with man; and evil spirits are such that they hold man in deadly hatred, and desire nothing so much as to destroy him both soul and body, and this they do in the case of those who have so indulged themselves in fantasies as to have separated from themselves the enjoyments proper to the natural man (HH 249).

People have contact with angels only when they are in innocence and humility. In the infancy of the human race, there was open communication with angels, and there will be again when we have regenerated to higher levels. "...To speak with the angels of heaven is granted only to those who are in truths from good,"[6] those who are already firm in their beliefs. At times we can be lifted out of the senses into a higher light:

> By means of his natural mind, raised to the light of heaven, man can think, yea, speak with angels; but the thought and speech of the angels then flow into the natural thought and speech of the man, and not conversely; so that angels speak with man in a natural language, which is the man's mother tongue. This is effected by a spiritual influx into what is natural, and not by any natural influx into what is spiritual. Human wisdom, which so long as man lives in the natural world is natural, can by no means be raised into angelic wisdom, but only into some image of it. The reason is that elevation of the natural mind is effected by continuity, as from shade to light, or from grosser to purer. Still the man in whom the spiritual degree has been opened comes into that wisdom when he dies; and he may also come into it by a suspension of bodily sensations, and then by an influx from above into the spiritual parts of his mind (DLW 257).

The latter sentence may have application to the place of spiritual meditation in the new age. Such meditation would not supersede the repentance and regeneration so clearly called for in the Writings, but would become a part of the overall process of rebirth.

Spirits with Us

> But the Spirit of the Lord departed from Saul, and an evil spirit from God troubled him....And so it was, whenever the spirit from God was upon Saul, that David would take a harp and play it with his hand. Then Saul would become refreshed and well, and the distressing spirit would depart from him (I Samuel 16:14,23).

Troubling spirits can attack all of us—driving us to anxiety, depression, even insanity—if we allow them. For instance:

As solicitude about things to come is what produces anxieties in man, and as such spirits appear in the region of the stomach, therefore anxieties affect the stomach more than the other viscera. It has also been given me to perceive how these anxieties are increased and diminished by the presence and removal of the spirits referred to.... When such anxieties take possession of the mind, the region about the stomach is constricted, and at times pain is felt there, and the anxieties also seem to rise up from there; and hence also it is that when man is no longer solicitous about the future, or when everything turns out well for him so that he no longer is fearful of any misfortune, the region about the stomach is relieved and expands, and he feels delight (AC 5178).

Bioenergetics is a form of therapy that works directly with the body to relieve specific tensions and deal with the emotions that arise from that release. The theory is that every tension has an emotional connection. The Writings certainly confirm a mind-body connection. The spirit-mind-body connection is even more powerful. Who has not felt anxiety in the pit of the stomach? It can be helpful to realize that there are spirits involved, because they do not like to be recognized; and to acknowledge their influx helps to dispel them.

Contrast that anxiety with this more enlightened approach:

Very different is the case with those who trust in the Divine. These, notwithstanding they have care for the morrow, still have it not, because they do not think of the morrow with solicitude, still less with anxiety. Unruffled is their spirit whether they obtain the objects of their desire, or not; and they do not grieve over the loss of them, being content with their lot. If they become rich, they do not set their hearts on riches; if they are raised to honors, they do not regard themselves as more worthy than others; if they become poor, they are not made sad; if their circumstances are mean, they are not dejected. They know that for those who trust in the Divine all things advance toward a happy state to eternity, and that whatever befalls them in time is still conducive thereto (AC 8478).

This kind of trust is the true meaning of 'taking no thought for the morrow.'

71

A common problem induced by spirits is preoccupation with petty concerns, i.e., "to think of my garden, of him who had the care of it, of my being called home, of money matters...."[7] Spirits will hold us in the treadmill of this kind of worry and "throw in inconvenient, troublesome, and evil suggestions ....These are the reflections of thought, in which whoever is detained [in them] he is the more infested by evil spirits the longer the reflection is continued."[8] From such infesting by evil spirits

> ...arises the melancholy of many persons, hence debilitated minds, hence the deliriums of many men, hence too insanities and fantasies....Some persons are led by spirits to that degree, that they cannot return to what is true, but their fantasies have become so deeply rooted, that as often as they fall into those thoughts, they are so completely absorbed in them that they cannot be dispelled by change of circumstances, but they remain in the persuasion that things are as they imagine, and themselves also. When cases of this kind are obvious to the world, they are called open insanities, for from such insanity or fantasy they do not suffer themselves to be recovered, though apparently sane on all other subjects, as many insane persons are (SD 3625-6).

Even with those who are mentally healthy initially, what begins as worry can lead to paranoia or insanity if unchecked. The line between emotional health and sickness can at times of trial seem very thin and indefinite. But the new Word reveals causes and liberating truths that can shed light on that line, and lead to thoughts and loves that dispel infesting thoughts and spirits.

To attempt to contact spirits is contrary to order for those on the spiritual path, opening them up to frightening dangers of possession by evil spirits. But there can be an awareness of good and evil spirits operating unconsciously upon our minds. This awareness, even though not specific, can be of real help in dispersing evil spirits and inviting heavenly ones.

> ...Evils cannot be removed unless they are sought out, discovered, acknowledged, confessed and resisted....The entire heaven is arranged in societies according to [affections of good, and the entire hell according to] the lusts of evil opposite to the affections of good. As to his spirit every man is in

some society; in a heavenly society if he is in an affection for good, but in an infernal society if he is in a lust of evil. This is unknown to man so long as he lives in the world; nevertheless he is in respect to his spirit in some society, and without this he cannot live, and by means of it he is governed by the Lord. If he is in an infernal society he can be led out of it by the Lord only in accordance with the laws of His Divine providence, among which is this, that the *man must see that he is there*, must wish to go out of it, and must try to do this of himself. This he can do while he is in the world, but not after death; for he then remains forever in the society into which he has inserted himself while in the world. This is the reason why man must examine himself, must recognize and acknowledge his sins and repent, and then must persevere to the end of his life (DP 278b:6; italics added).

This does not mean having our spiritual eyes opened and seeing a society in hell; rather it means acknowledging or seeing in our understanding that the evil love of that society is lodged in one's heart, and then praying to leave that terrible inner state.

Initiative

I will lift up my hand in Your name (Psalm 63:4).

Even if we are mentally healthy, we are not necessarily 'unruffled in spirit'! It is still possible to be undermined by distressing spirits and wrong attitudes. How can we defend ourselves to maintain spiritual and emotional health?

In times of surpassing trial or terrible sorrow the Lord draws near. The more penetrating the trouble, the nearer we, in our spirit, are brought to the sun of heaven. When there is the death of one deeply loved the Lord removes us from our natural cycle of states. He opens up within our hearts the remains implanted in infancy and childhood which are above consciousness and entirely forgotten in ordinary states.

In exceptional need, the Lord permits an influx from these interior innocent affections that temporarily breaks the veil between heaven and earth, awakening us out of our spiritual sleep. Then we are with the angels in our hearts, in the protection of their sphere. Although we are not always consciously aware of it, there is this opening of remains when there is a need. When there is fatal illness or utter sorrow, the Lord leads us "beside the still waters," and "into the green pastures" of the spirit.

This happens sometimes in societies as a whole, in nations. The demands and needs of past world wars have to some degree opened up a special influx from heaven, counterbalancing the spheres of hell and death. The soldier going to battle is poignantly aware of life; myriad things become sweet and alive that in ordinary states are taken for granted. And with the family left behind an interior influx often opens up that brings a trust in the Lord; a sure faith that providence is acting for eternal ends. Even a whole nation rises to the challenge of war, coming into states of unity and dedication—of selflessness—that seldom exist.

The Lord opens up our remains in times of deep need because otherwise spiritual equilibrium would be broken and we would be in immediate danger of destruction by the hells. It is a Divine law that we are kept in spiritual equilibrium between heaven and hell. The powers of hell that operate on us are balanced out by an equally strong influx of heavenly power. In this way there is always freedom.

Times of exceptional natural trial, such as war, sickness or death, bring starkly before us the issues of life. For then things deeply treasured by the natural mind are taken away. Natural attachments, natural health and peace, are threatened. In such times, part of us would rise up to challenge the Lord, to question and reject His providence, letting evil spirits flow in.[9] Without immediate help, all would then be over with our spirit. To maintain spiritual equilibrium, the Lord must open up special avenues of heavenly influx.

When we are in deep trial, what we need, what our spirits pray for, is heavenly love. For all the answers to life are in such unselfish love from the Lord. And this is what the Lord awakens when He awakens the remains of childhood. Within these is celestial love, the love of others more than ourselves. And this is married to a host of truths sparkling with life.

Yet times of exceptional natural sorrow are usually few in our lifetimes; the awakening of remains is a rare thing. What sustains us in our more ordinary routine and trials? How does the Lord help in the ordinary temptations of the spirit—ordinary in one sense but so difficult in another? The law for the Divine help is the same: spiritual equilibrium is jealously guarded by the Divie providence. The Lord is nearer to us in temptation than at any other time. According to the need, so is the closeness.[10]

But this does not mean that we should wait, with hands down, for the Lord to draw near with a special saving influx. Taking initiative is also our responsibility. "I will lift up my hands in Your name."

> There are certain spirits, who during their life in the world, because they had been told that all good is from the Lord, and that a man can do nothing of himself, had held it as a principle not to compel themselves in anything, but to cease from all effort; thinking that . . . all effort would be in vain; and therefore they had waited for immediate influx into the effort of their will, and did not compel themselves to do anything good, going so far that when anything evil crept in, as they felt no resistance from within, they resigned themselves to it also, supposing that it was permissible to do so. But these spirits are as it were devoid of what is their own, so that they have no determination to anything, and are therefore among the more useless. For they suffer themselves to be led alike by the evil and by the good, and suffer much from the evil. But they who have compelled themselves to resist what is evil and false . . . these in the other life cannot be led by evil spirits, but are among the happy (AC 1937:2,3).

Initiative in spiritual things is in our hands, although we should recognize the power to take it is from the Lord. When challenges confront us, we should go to the Lord and to the Word and pray for help and enlightenment. But then we should *act*, as when Moses stood before the Red Sea, with the army of Pharaoh poised behind the Israelites. "The Lord said to Moses, Why do you cry to Me? Tell the children of Israel to go forward."[11]

To lift up our hands to the Lord means to let the Lord lead us—to compel ourselves to obey the Word, for the Word is God. In contrast to this, we are quite capable of taking initiative from other motives—from pride or conceit, for instance. But then our hands are not raised to God; they are raised in self adulation. In this case, we will fail when the most vicious devils attack. The saying that 'the Lord helps those who help themselves' can be misleading. We can help ourselves from wrong motives, but the Lord helps those who take initiative *"in His name."* Only the Lord can withstand the attack of the lowest hells; we can only triumph when we ask the Lord to fight for us.

When the Amalekites attacked the children of Israel in the wilderness, Moses was told to ascend a nearby hill to raise his arms when the battle started. As long as his hands were raised, the children of Israel would win. The battle started the next day and they conquered until Moses' strength failed—until his hands lowered—then the Amalekites quickly turned the tide of battle in their favor.

In the spiritual sense, Moses corresponds to Divine truth in us, especially in the Writings; and his lifting his hands to the Lord represents our leading ourselves to obey Divine truth. We do this from the hilltop of love given through remains. However, the spiritual person cannot continuously and without rest fight from highest revealed truth without being overcome by spiritual exhaustion:

> By Israel now conquering, and now Amalek, was represented that they who are of the spiritual church cannot be in a faith that continuously looks to the Lord, but that they are by turns in a faith which looks to themselves and the world. For they who are of that church are in obscurity, and consequently in weakness as to faith (AC 8607).

We need more than our highest ideals in prolonged temptations. If we fight from these *only*, eventually we yield to the lowest hells from exhaustion. The war with the Amalekites represents those most miserable temptations that go on and on, seemingly endlessly. When we begin to lose our spiritual strength, it is the lowest or Amalekite devils who suddenly and indirectly insinuate despair, who lead us to think our whole life has been worthless. Their hope is to lead us on to complete yielding—that is, to spiritual death and if possible they would lead us to natural death too—to suicide. They come at times when trials combine: when spiritual *and* natural temptation together undermine us, when we feel let down by the church, by friends, by life itself.

The stone upon which Moses rested represents "Divine truth in the ultimate of order."[12] When we find our spiritual strength failing, we can turn to the truth in the letter of the Word, the Old and New Testaments, for support. The heart can rest upon such passages as the Lord's prayer, certain psalms and commandments. And if there is vacillation and doubt, the Ten Commandments provide their enduring childhood sphere of love and obedience to the Lord. They are the Lord's commands: "You shall have no other gods before Me.... You shall not commit adultery.... You shall not steal." However if it is not Divine command, but trust and love of the Lord that are needed, there are songs such as the 23rd and 139th psalms and teachings such as the two great commandments: "You shall love the Lord your God with all your heart, with all your soul, and with all your mind.... You shall love your neighbor as yourself."[13]

The rock Moses sat upon also represents ultimate truth in practice. There is support and encouragement in the very routine of one's work, in useful, external acts. Sometimes in spiritually disturbed states, it really helps to turn deliberately to orderly physical acts such as the chores of caring for one's house and belongings. These can help still the mind's confusions and fears and bring something of order and peace.

As Moses rested upon the rock, Aaron and Hur upheld his hands. They represent here "lower truths in successive order relative to the truth that is the first of order, which is represented by Moses."[14] The inner guide during regeneration is ideals of truth from the Word. However, supporting these ideals are many levels of truth, derived from parents, teachers and the world around us. These lesser truths support our highest ideals and help us endure with patience the struggle of temptations. Aaron and Hur include a vast panorama of forms and truths that support and strengthen our belief in the Lord. They represent our perception of beauty in nature, art, music, song—in every realm where imagination is combined with grace. This is the grace of form that confirms the Lord's presence in His realms of creation. The sciences that speak of the Lord's omniscience and omnipotence—these also are Aaron and Hur, upholding the arms of Moses.

Humanly, Aaron and Hur represent friendship, for friends keep alive what is human or innocent in us and they hold up our hands. Shyness and inhibition can lead us away from helping friends and place us on an island of loneliness. Yet we are made for each other; we need human contact, warmth and support.

When temptations are severe, almost unbearable, the promise of Moses on the hilltop can give us courage and hope. There he rested on the rock his hands upheld by Aaron and Hur. And his hands were steady until victory! Behind this spiritually is the Lord Himself, inviting us to His arms. We are given truths in the Writings to help shield us from disturbing spirits; and we are kept in a balance between good and evil influences so that we are in the freedom to be our true selves. The angels with us provide the golden thread of remains, to help us on our path:

> These things the angels do from the love they have from the Lord for they perceive nothing more delightful and happy than to remove evils from a man, and lead him to hea- ven . . . . Scarcely any man believes that the Lord takes such care of a man, and this continually from the first thread of his life to the last of it, and afterward to eternity (AC 5992).

"Do Unto Others"

My soul thirsts for You;
My flesh longs for You
In a dry and thirsty land
Where there is no water (Psalm 63:1).

The initiative that we take to defend ourselves against disturbing spirits can normally work beautifully for us. But what if we find ourselves caught in a web of emotional or mental illness? Are we then in freedom to choose the spirits with us? If we become ruled by emotions beyond our control, are we still free or are we at the mercy of negative spirits?

There is hope in the knowledge that we have some choice about which spirits affect us. Perhaps, sometime in early child- hood, we 'chose' thoughts and feelings that grew into emotional or mental disorders. We did this unconsciously, as a reaction and defense against hurt or trauma. If we can be led *back* to the point where that pivotal choice or choices occurred, the wound can be opened and cleansed so that it can begin to heal. This involves the courage to look at, to feel, what is so painful to us.

The Lord is the Divine Physician. There is not an illness, physical or mental, that is not open to eventual healing. Cures for some diseases may take centuries to be discovered but they *will* come, as they always come now after death. Wholeness of spirit, mind and body is a goal of the Lord's providence. It could not be otherwise in the Lord's compassion. He showed this compassion in Gadara, when He cured the man frighteningly possessed by evil spirits. Jesus was not afraid; He did not turn His back. Instead He went directly to that man and helped him.

His action is an example for us, not to turn away from those with emotional or mental problems but rather to show compassion—not a pseudo-compassion coming from a sense of superiority but a genuine caring for another human being. We need to help and search for the truths that heal. And above all is the need for the open friendship of caring and wanting to help someone we love, for such love is the Lord's love.

Chapter 7

Healing in His Wings

For He said to him, "Come out of the man, unclean spirit!"
Then He asked him, "What is your name?" And he answered, saying, "My name is Legion; for we are many." And
he begged Him earnestly that He would not send them out of
the country. Now a large herd of swine was feeding there
near the mountains. And all the demons begged Him, saying, "Send us to the swine, that we may enter them." And at
once Jesus gave them permission. Then the unclean spirits
went out and entered the swine (there were about two thousand); and the herd ran violently down the steep place into
the sea, and drowned in the sea (Mark 5:8-13).

Emotional disorders can be healed, either here or in the
spiritual world. The Lord comes to everyone, if we invite Him,
as He came to the Gadarene. He drives out the legion of fears
and anger from where they have been buried within us so that
we can see that they are like perverted swine. Then we can
finally begin to be free of them and become truly human.

But we tend to resist exposing negative feelings. Hatred,
anxiety and the killing instinct are less than animal-like desires,
low on the human scale. We would rather keep them tucked
away from view, and the spirits behind them would also rather
not be exposed. So our defenses are up.

'Swine' are the lowest type of spirits such as the 'conscience
mongers,' haters, and killers. The demons emerging and entering the swine represent these spirits surfacing into the conscious
mind by the Lord's power. Once we are made aware of them,
we can perceive their swine-like quality. If this is clearly seen,
the next step is casting these emotions into the sea of hell, which
the Lord does. With the swine of Gadara it was done quickly,
but psychological healing can take many years.

However, we cannot just blame emotional problems on spirits and leave it at that. We have to find the roots in ourselves, in our subjective feelings, that allow those particular spirits to cling to us. This means uncovering whatever pain it was that warped our original love and perception. Recognizing the spirits' influence can help us to see the transmitters of negative emotions. But that does not bring us to the original cause in ourselves of such emotions. We need to search within to reach our own emotional core.

Why do we have to go through the wrenching experience of having our raw, horrible feelings exposed? Why can't we just solve our problems by understanding them? On the spiritual level, *Divine Providence* explains:

> It would have been possible for the Lord to heal the understanding in every man, and thus cause him to think what is good and not what is evil, and this by fears of various kinds, by miracles, by conversations with the dead, and by visions and dreams. But to heal the understanding alone is to heal man only from without; for the understanding with its thought is the external of man's life, while the will with its affection is the internal of his life; consequently the healing of the understanding alone would be like palliative healing, whereby the interior malignity, shut in and wholly prevented from going out, would destroy first the near and then the remote parts, even till the whole would become dead (DP 282).

On the external level of the mind, our feelings are stronger than our thoughts, which flow from feelings. We need to bring to consciousness the emotional roots of problems. If our outer understanding alone were healed, we "would become like a dead body embalmed or encased in fragrant aromatics and roses."[1] The deeper loves and emotions must be discovered—they are what bring the mind to life.

Thoughts flow from feelings and should not be dammed up. If our thoughts flow freely, we can know our inner nature. Being clear and honest about who we are is the first step to changing ourselves for the better. If our thoughts could not flow freely from our life's love, we would not be human since our "two faculties called liberty and rationality, in which the essential humanity consists, would be destroyed."[2] Seeing that our thoughts are from negative emotions does *not* mean confirming or justifying them. It means really *seeing* them so that they and their emotions can be removed from power:

> ... a love of evil that is not seen is like an enemy in ambush, like matter in an ulcer, like poison in the blood, or corruption in the breast, which, if they are kept shut in, induce death. But on the other hand, if man is permitted to think about the evils of his life's love, even so far as to intend them, they can be cured by spiritual means, as diseases are by natural means.... Man is free to think as he pleases, to the end that his life's love may come forth from its lurking places into the light of his understanding... (DP 281).

This passage deals with spiritual illness using natural symbols. Emotional and mental disorders are also like an infection; they have to be exposed and treated before they cause emotional death. A problem, spiritual or emotional, has to be seen as a problem before it can be uprooted. Sometimes this can be done by honest reflection and self-appraisal. But sometimes a therapist is needed to help us when we feel unable to make real progress on our own.

A painful question often arises if emotional disorder comes upon someone when it was never detected or experienced before. Sometimes the depression or tension is so severe that one comes to his or her wit's end and does not know where to turn. If religious faith is strong, there may be a strong aversion to going into therapy. Isn't faith enough to meet all emergencies? Don't the Writings give the clear answer to every question of life? To turn to psychotherapy seems like a terrible fall from trust. Perhaps only necessity—that is the fear of losing sanity—will force one into this step.

But this is so unfair to the great numbers of truly caring mental therapists. A genuine therapist cares as much about healing the mind as does a priest about healing the ills of the spirit. Although there are people involved in mental health care who are atheists and charlatans, this is true also of every profession, including the ministry! But, there are also caring and compassionate workers in the mental health professions whose joy is to bring gradual healing to hurt minds and emotions. The

Writings themselves speak implicitly of the value of seeking counsel in therapy-like situations.[3]

It is important to know that in the various schools of psychotherapy there are those who honor the basic, valid belief system of a client, and those who are cold toward such a system. Those who seek help should enquire and choose a therapist in harmony with their basic value systems.

Bitter feelings are brought to light in therapy so that they no longer spill over with devastating harm into daily life. If anger towards a parent is revealed, for instance, it is less likely to be passed on to a child in the form of hidden or open child abuse. A powerful realization of the origin of the hatred can help when the old anger is aroused by a child. It might hold one back from striking out blindly.

Confessions are powerful. The Lord asked, "What ails you, Hagar?"[4] He already knew the answer but one of the reasons He asks such questions is so that people "may have consolations from being able to express their feelings, which often brings relief."[5] This idea has been a cornerstone of therapy since the days of Freud. Releasing feelings brings the first taste of well-being.

There is relief in this, but emotional growth is not always painless. We may feel strong anguish as defenses crumble and hidden 'devils' emerge. New insights fight with old feelings and we get caught in the middle. The possibility of a whole new outlook on life emerges and that can be frightening. The boundaries of who we are change. We grieve as old securities, old defenses, are exposed and lost. However "grief by degrees diminishes, and at last vanishes away. It is as with a weak and sickly body, which is to be restored to health by painful means; in this state, at first it has grief."[6]

It takes courage and self-compulsion to face ourselves honestly. We try to discover many ways of dodging the process. It sometimes takes years of searching, one hard-won breakthrough after another, before health comes. However:

> ...in all self-compulsion to what is good there is a certain freedom.... For instance, ... in one who is willing to suffer bodily pain for the sake of health, there is a willingness and

thus a certain freedom from which the man acts, although the dangers and the pains, while he is in them, take away his perception of this willingness or freedom...(AC 1937:4).

Within the struggle is the liberating sense of real growth. The pain feels better than prolonging the inner stagnation and numbness. Sometimes we may feel as if our world is shattering and it would be better to be back in a safe hole. Yet deep within us there is a sense of dawning aliveness instead of emotional death. This feeling of life comes from having freely chosen to face our feelings, and from an openness to the Lord as the healer and giver of life and love.

The swine of Gadara were on a hill, which corresponds to charity and love. If negative emotions are exposed while we are in a state of charity, we can realize that they have been ruling us. When they emerge they run wild because malicious spirits cannot tolerate the presence of good for long. They dash themselves down from the hill of remains within us; and our false emotional self dies with them.

When the people of Gadara heard about the swine, they came to investigate. They were astonished to see the man who had been possessed sitting with Jesus, clothed and in his right mind. This frightened them so that they asked Jesus to leave. The cured man begged to go with Him, but Jesus told him to "go home to your friends, and tell them what great things the Lord has done for you, and how He has had compassion on you." The Gadarene did this "and all marveled."[7]

If we have suffered the internal possession of emotional disorder or mental illness, we can go through a similar healing experience. When the worst feelings within us surface and we let go of them, we are left free to grow spiritually. A profound change can come over us. When the disorder is healed, the genuine person behind the turmoil can emerge and really begin to live. This may be hard for others to believe at first, but the inner peace of sanity speaks for itself. This cure may take many states and years to be accomplished. The man at Gadara had been long possessed. But the miracle is that the cure is there!

We can begin to feel forgiving towards those who caused us pain. Forgiveness is a spiritual balm; it is honest and powerfully healing. Parents or others may have harmed us, but we are not free of the same trespass. Haven't we harmed others, maybe even our own children? The Lord's prayer has a liberating key to spiritual and mental health: "forgive us our trespasses, as we forgive those who trespass against us."

The question of 'blame' is a difficult one in approaching genuine mental health. If hurts have come through parents, and therapy or self-examination discloses this reality, what attitude do we take towards the one who has hurt us? If we are honestly going to face all the emotions involved, the first step is to recognize that we have attached a terribly strong blame to the parent or surrogate involved. Our love for them would deny this, and close over this blaming. But honesty, and real healing, involve facing the reality of the hurt, the hate and the blame.

But the next step is to look at ourselves honestly. Are we entirely innocent? Every infant is born with hereditary evil. If there has been a trauma in early childhood, perhaps even an unintended hurt by a parent, the hereditary nature of the infant will fasten on that hurt. It will flow in with hate, loving to nurse the hate. There is a joy, from hell, in blaming others. Therefore it is valuable to go back in self-examination, and to face honestly our own role in nursing a trauma that has damaged our psyche. Parents, through evil unconscious to themselves, or because of their own emotional disorders, may have inflicted harm on a child when it is the last thing they would knowingly do.

In the final analysis, the only real blame is from hell if there has been self-examination and shunning of evil from trust in the Lord by all the parties involved. Evil and the harm that it does is from hell. If we would ascribe all evil to hell and all good to the Lord, we would be on the path to true spiritual freedom and the highest reality.[8]

If there is to be final healing, the question of blame must be resolved. The hate and anger against a parent must be honestly confessed to oneself. The joy in casting blame should be seen for what it is—a nursing of what is selfish. At the same time, it is right to feel zeal against any evil that has been inflicted. A strong example of this would be in child abuse. The child must be able to feel zeal against the terrible evil involved, or else he or she will never be freed. Zeal is a genuine, protective, spiritual love; the Lord Himself felt it when He cleansed the temple in Jerusalem. In the final steps of healing, this is a zeal against hell itself.

All this paves the way for the inmost of life, which is heavenly love itself—caring, unselfish love to flow into the mind and heart of the one who is being healed. Spiritual love heals, and restores life.[9] This love must come, if forgiveness is to have complete impact and meaning. To forgive is truly human—and Divine! At last we can be free, like the Gadarene, to love and serve God.

Body and Mind

To him who overcomes I will give some of the hidden manna to eat (Revelation 2:17).

All of the healing mentioned in the Word refers on a deeper level to spiritual healing. For instance, "I will heal them and reveal to them the abundance of peace and truth"[10] speaks of removing evil emotions and thoughts, and replacing them with love and truth. The inner beauty of the Word is its spiraling, correspondential levels of meaning. In ourselves are the levels of body, natural mind, spiritual mind and soul.

According to *Divine Providence*,[11] one of the causes of emotional/mental disorders is a sick body. Healing in this case can be approached on the physical level. Life flows down from the Lord through the spiritual world and becomes tangible to us on this earthly plane. The Writings often stress the power of 'ultimates' or the objects of our senses which contain life from above:

> For all the organic forms in man are compounded of more interior forms, and these again of forms still more interior, and so on to the inmost: by means of these, communication with all the affection and thought of man's mind is made possible. For a man's mind, in each separate part of it, extends into all things of his body; it is into all things of the body that its range of activity is, for it is the very form of life. Unless the mind had that field, there would not be a mind, nor a man. It is in consequence of the above that the choice and good pleasure of a man's will instantly bring forth and

determine actions, altogether as if the thought and will were themselves in the things of the body, instead of being above them (DLDW 40).

The connections between the body, mind, and soul work so smoothly that we are not usually aware of the degrees; they form a whole working unit. What we do on the physical plane affects levels far above our consciousness. This idea can have powerful applications to our daily lives, for example the use and abuse of alcohol, food, and drugs.

If we change our external world, over which we have some control, the Lord can improve our inner self. Jesus washed his disciples' feet, saying, " 'What I am doing you do not understand now, but you will know after this.' Peter said to Him, 'You shall never wash my feet!' Jesus answered him, 'If I do not wash you, you have no part with Me.' "[12] Spiritually, "the internal cannot be cleansed from the lusts of evil so long as the evils in the external man are not put away, since these obstruct."[13] This would also apply to some extent to the physical or bodily level. If our bodies are healed, this will have an effect on our minds:

> ...One who is in merely external pleasures, makes much of himself, indulges his stomach, loves to live sumptuously, and makes the height of pleasure to consist in eatables and drinkables. One who is in internal things also finds pleasure in these things, but his ruling affection is to nourish his body with food pleasurably for the sake of its health, to the end that he may have a sound mind in a sound body, thus chiefly for the sake of the health of the mind, to which the health of the body serves as a means. One who is a spiritual man does not rest here, but regards the health of the mind or soul as a means for the acquisition of intelligence and wisdom—not for the sake of reputation, honors and gain—but for the sake of the life after death. One who is spiritual in a more interior degree regards intelligence and wisdom as a mediate end having for its object that he may serve as a useful member in the Lord's kingdom; and one who is a celestial man, that he may serve the Lord. To such a one bodily food is a means for the enjoyment of spiritual food, and spiritual food is a means for the enjoyment of celestial food; and as they ought to serve

in this manner, these foods also correspond, and are therefore called foods (AC 4459:6).

This passage shows the spiral ascending through degrees from the lower to the highest levels. Keeping the body healthy creates a clear receptacle for the natural mind and spiritual mind. This does not mean that we should become obsessive about our bodies. They are a means to a higher end, not an end in themselves. They are created for a higher use.

Use

Return, O Lord!
How long?
And have compassion on Your servants...
Make us glad according to the days in which you have afflicted us...
Let Your work appear to Your servants.
And Your glory to their children.
And let the beauty of the Lord our God be upon us,
And establish the work of our hands for us;
Yes, establish the work of our hands (Psalm 90:13-17).

In *Conjugial Love* there is a story about spirits newly arrived from earth who believed that they would sit on thrones with Christ and be waited upon by angels. They were allowed to live out this fantasy. They were robed and jewelled and enthroned. Heralds came and told them to wait awhile for palaces that were being prepared in heaven for them.

They waited and waited until their spirits panted for breath and they were utterly wearied with eager longing. After three hours heaven was opened above their heads, and angels looked down and having compassion on them said, "Why do you sit so foolish and take an actor's part? They have been playing tricks upon you, and have changed you from men to idols, because you have set your hearts upon the idea that you are to reign with Christ as kings and princes, and are to be ministered unto by the angels. Have you forgotten the Lord's words, that he who would be great in heaven must become a servant? Learn then what is meant by kings and princes, and by reigning with Christ, that it is to be wise and perform uses; for the kingdom of Christ, which is heaven, is a kingdom of uses. For the Lord loves all, and from love wills good to all, and good is use" (CL 7).

The angels then gave the spirits a true idea of prestige and heaven. After listening to reason, the 'kings' came down from their thrones and threw away their scepters, crowns and robes. Then "the mist wherein was the aura of fantasy departed from them, and a bright cloud overveiled them wherein was an aura of wisdom, whereby sanity was restored to their minds."[14]

Angels do not lead an idle life at all. They love to do good for others; it is essential to their nature. "Good is use."[15] The angels work together in beautiful harmony and unity. Heaven is composed of myriads of angels, in the same way that a human body is composed of cells:

> ... there is in each single part in the human body, by virtue of the use it serves, something typical of the whole (*universum*); for each part regards the "whole" there as its own on which it depends, while the "whole" regards each part as its own, by means of which it has its existence .... In spiritual thought a man is not a person but a use, for spiritual thought does not include any idea of person, any more than of matter, space and time; accordingly when in heaven any one sees another, he sees him, certainly, as a man, but he thinks of him as a use (DLDW 40).

Angels love to perform uses for the whole of creation, and they love what they do because their uses are perfectly suited to their abilities and temperaments. People here on earth who have worked at jobs they don't quite fit into can really understand how this would be heavenly. The angels' work flows creatively from their inner loves, and they feel a unity with the whole, extremely alive as givers and receivers: "it is the delight of every one in heaven to share his delights and blessings with others; and as such is the character of all that are in the heavens it is clear how immeasurable is the delight of heaven."[16] Every angel's use is an integral part of the whole, without the sense of being a tiny cog in an impersonal wheel.

> There were some spirits who believed from an opinion adopted in the world that heavenly happiness consists in an idle life in which they would be served by others; but they

were told that happiness never consists in abstaining from work and getting satisfaction therefrom. This would mean every one's desiring the happiness of others for himself, and what every one wished for, no one would have. Such a life would be an idle not an active life, and would stupefy all the powers of life; and every one ought to know that without activity of life there can be no happiness of life, and that rest from this activity should be only for the sake of recreation, that one may return with more vigor to the activity of his life. They were then shown by many evidences that angelic life consists in performing the good works of charity, which are uses, and that the angels find all their happiness in use, from use, and in accordance with use (HH 403).

Uses can be very healing to us on earth. "A man is not of sound mind unless use is his affection, or unless he occupies himself with use."[17] The mind becomes oriented by use into a form that is truly human.[18] The only remedy for the spiritually insane in the other world is to work![19] This does not mean that life should be all work and no play; recreation is also useful.[20] In fact, "everything that [good] love does it calls use."[21] Striving to love to do good for others creates a harmony in our lives. Our outer lives become an extension of our inner love and charity.

We have internal and external thoughts. "A man is in external thought when in the society of others, whether he is then listening or speaking , or teaching, or engaged in some action; he is in external thought, too, when writing."[22] Internal thoughts come from what a person is really feeling when at home and giving free scope to his interior affection.[23] After death we gradually leave the plane of external thoughts, and become outwardly who we really are inside. We become the exact image of our internal thoughts:

The man who is of sound mind will then see and hear wonderful things; he will hear and see that many people who in the world used to speak wisely or preach skillfully, or teach learnedly, or write with knowledge and who acted, too, with prudence, begin, as soon as the external of their mind has been withdrawn, to think, speak and act in such a senseless fashion that no maniac in the world would do so more insanely...(DLDW 43).

Our genuine intentions are what count. If we are sincerely working towards loving the Lord and the goal of wholeness, we will be cured after death of natural and spiritual imbalance. In contrast to this, those who seem sane to others, but are privately full of hatred, will be exposed. It is better to work these things through now, not out of fear, but out of love to the Lord and friends. In the other life our motives and inner, private thoughts are laid bare.

Wholeness means being well on every level, so that these levels perform together in unity. This happens through use.

> All... who in the world have loved uses, and done them from love of them, think sanely in their spirit, and their spirit thinks sanely in their body, for in this way their interior thought is their exterior thought also, and through this latter their speech is from their interior thought, so also is their action. Affection for use has kept their mind in that affection and has not allowed it to stray away...(DLDW 46).

When we are doing useful work, we feel more creative and alive. It also helps take our minds off our problems. This doesn't mean being a workaholic to avoid facing ourselves. We have to face our fears, anger and evils before we can sincerely love what we do. Then, performing a use for others can fulfill our lives. More than this, it can lead to a home, an eternal living use, in heaven. "In My Father's house there are many mansions; if it were not so I would have told you."[24]

Which Way?

> Unto you who fear My name
> The sun of righteousness shall arise
> With healing in His wings (Malachi 4:2).

> "The Sun of righteousness" signifies the good of love, which is the celestial Divine; and the "wings of Jehovah, in which there is healing," signify truth from that good, which is the spiritual Divine; "healing" is reformation thereby (AE 283b:9).

There are many approaches to healing and many ways of understanding mental health (Freudian, Jungian, Adlerian, behaviorist, gestalt, etc.). Emotional disorders may arise from hurt in infancy, from the body, from spirits, from a combination of these, or from other causes. Illness and healing come in many different forms. If we become stuck in one theory, we may lose the balance that other perspectives can bring. Holistic healing can include many levels of approach. The search for cogent healing methods will continue, and out of this will come clearer concepts and more unifying principles than we have today.

Although emotional disorders are on the natural level, we can also search for healing in a spiritual way. We can apply spiritual truths to the natural plane by looking to the higher levels with an open mind and heart, and then seeing applications. What happens to us on earth is a foundation and a form for what is happening to us spiritually. As we grow to wholeness on the natural level, we can receive increasing influx of life and light from the spiritual level of our minds. Through reformation and regeneration, inner levels can be healed of their spiritual illnesses, and with this comes bliss and peace we cannot imagine now.

Psychology is still in its infancy. There are vast areas to be explored intertwining religious and psychological ideas; we are only beginning to touch the possibilities. The Writings promise that humanity will progress into higher spiritual development, following the golden thread from our race's infancy to the innocence and wisdom of enlightenment of a new golden age. It is wonderful to think of the healing that will come to the whole human race as this gradual process unfolds.

And He showed me a pure river of the water of life clear as crystal, proceeding from the throne of God and of the Lamb. In the middle of its street, and on either side of the river, was the tree of life, which bore twelve fruits, each tree yielding its fruit every month. And the leaves of the tree were for the healing of the nations (Revelation 22:1,2).

Part II

****
Spiritual Health
****

Chapter 8

The Divine Promise

Jesus said, "When I am lifted up from the earth, I will draw all peoples to Myself" (John 12:32).

There is actually a sphere proceeding continually from the Lord and filling the entire spiritual and natural worlds which raises all towards heaven. It is like a strong current in the ocean, which unobservedly draws a vessel (TCR 652:3).

The plan in this section of the book is to unfold the universal states of spiritual growth symbolized by the life stories of the patriarchs: Abraham, Isaac, Jacob and Joseph. Then towards the end there is a chapter on the psychological stages of growth that can support and underpin spiritual rebirth. The final chapter is on the Lord as our father and only God.

The process of spiritual growth, even with its times of trial, is full of inner delights. Before we proceed on this inner journey it is hard to even imagine the peace and joy that are possible, especially if we are caught in an emotional disorder. However, God is always drawing us upwards towards eternal happiness. "The Lord's Divine providence has as its end a heaven from the human race.... Heaven is conjunction with the Lord.... The more nearly a man is conjoined with the Lord the happier he becomes."[1] If we allow it, we can be drawn by the current of love into joy in eternal use.

Heaven is a place of astonishing joy—inward bliss that courses through every heartbeat of the angels, and is infilled and filled again in the creativity of uses. Their happiness is such that Swedenborg simply could not describe it adequately. The love and joy of an angel are so intense that they move even hardened spirits.

THE DIVINE PROMISE

STAGES OF LIFE		
I	ABRAM/ABRAHAM INNOCENCE - CHILDHOOD	THY WILL BE DONE, AS IN HEAVEN, SO UPON THE EARTH
II	ISHMAEL/ISAAC LOVE OF TRUTH/IDEALS - YOUNG ADULT	
III	JACOB/ISRAEL TRUTH APPLIED TO LIFE - MIDDLE YEARS	
IV	JOSEPH DISCOVERING THE LORD DIRECTLY - OLD AGE	

We feel something of this angelic delight in childhood, especially secretly and tenderly in infancy, flowing in from the innocence and peace of the highest angels. If we do not lose this joy by deliberately turning against it as an adult, then it gives us ultimate security. The highest angels are with us in that delight, and no evil spirit can come near it.

The tremendous happiness felt on occasions in childhood is not wiped out upon entering adult life. Remains are withdrawn deep within for their protection, but they constantly attempt to inflow; and, if we look to the Lord, there will be times when they return. Even among the cares and trials of our daily lives, we can become aware of our Heavenly Father's care for us, and experience a sense of peace and trust in Him. "Those who dwell under His shadow shall return."[2] As long as we shun harmful tendencies the joy of heaven filters through in various ways.

The Word gives the impression that God feels negative emotions, saying that He is angry, or takes vengeance, hates, damns, punishes, casts into hell, and tempts, "all of which pertain to evil, and therefore are evils."[3] These are appearances, adopted for the needs of more childlike states of mind. The truth within is "that the Lord is never angry, never takes vengeance, never hates, damns, punishes, casts into hell or tempts."[4] "The Lord imputes good to every man, but hell imputes evil to every man."[5]

"... The Lord cannot do evil to any man, consequently He cannot impute evil to man; for He is love itself and mercy itself, thus good itself."[6] There are spirits, such as the 'conscience mongers,' who kill spiritual delight. Hedonistic spirits fixate us on joy or gratification apart from use, which destroys genuine happiness. We should not confuse harmful spirits with the Lord or the angels, who only want us to be truly happy.

As far as is honestly possible the Lord wants life on earth to be happy. We "need not go about like a devotee with a sad and sorrowful countenance and drooping head, but may be joyful and cheerful."[7] Within the process of spiritual growth is the seed of heavenly joy that grows as we progress. This especially comes when we realize that after death we will live spiritually in a heavenly body in a world of astounding beauty. To reach true happiness, we have to turn to God and to the path of spiritual rebirth.

99

The Vision

Then Jehovah appeared to Abram and said, "To your descendants I will give this land," And there he built an altar to the Lord, who had appeared to him (Genesis 12:7).

"Jehovah appeared to Abram," signifies that Jehovah appeared to the Lord while yet a child; "and said, 'To your descendants I will give this land,' " signifies that celestial things should be given to those who should have faith in Him; "And there he built an altar to the Lord, who had appeared to him," signifies the first worship of His Father from the celestial of love (AC 1445).

The Lord on earth was glorified, or made Divine, in the same way that we are regenerated, or made angelic. He showed us the path, and gave us a Divine example. God always wants to share His life of love and wisdom with us. He has a promise for us that is unfolded in the life stories of the patriarchs Abraham, Isaac, Jacob and Joseph. The inmost joys of these men, the direct promises to them by Jehovah, and their struggles and discoveries have direct application to each of our lives. There is a universal theme about each patriarch that sums up what the Lord offers us in human life.

With Abram there is innocence: a willingness to leave Haran at the call of the Lord, and go into Canaan, the land of celestial love, a pastoral land. Here are the groves of trees where Jehovah is met, and the mountains of Judah, where celestial love is discovered. These are the eternal hills. Then there is the promise of Egypt, and the later visions in Canaan stretching to all eternity, given by Jehovah to Abraham. Abraham represents childhood remains, and these are eternal with the good; they are the father of all to come.

With Isaac there is laughter: not mocking laughter, but the sheer joy of the discovery of Divine truth. There is conjugial love: Isaac's discovery of Rebekah and her discovery of him. Constantly in his life he dwells by wells of water where he finds oases of delight. This patriarch represents the adult perception of Divine truth, and the inner happiness this brings.

With Jacob there is struggle—even at his birth—but there is the birthright and the blessing by his father. The Divine dream appears to Jacob at Beth-el, with the ladder stretching up to the Lord in heaven, and the angels of God ascending and descending upon it. In Padan-aram he finds Rachel, and marries her after marrying Leah. Gradually there is a mellowing with Jacob. He becomes very different and sees that Laban is no longer with him. Jacob returns home to meet and wrestle the angel, and to have his name changed to Israel. This is the major stage of life when heaven would come even to our natural life—first with real struggle to obey the Lord, but then with a gradual mellowing.

Finally, there is Joseph: "This dreamer is coming!"[8] His life is the story of the celestial state we can attain in old age: the celestial that was thought to be dead, killed by a wild beast, but is protected by the Lord. This is the celestial quality that can marvelously explain dreams and is raised to leadership. This celestial is finally recognized and loved by all his spiritual brothers. In the end, Joseph is inmost love released: the deepest reality and wonder of human life. This is true love of the Lord, of use, and of our marriage partner.

Spiritually, we are all descendants of Abram. God promises us that if we turn to Him, we will feel the celestial love of heaven. The unfolding of spiritual growth from Abraham to Joseph is not forced on us. There is no unyielding predestination within it. The wonderful gifts which the Lord offers in the spiritual sense of the stories of the patriarchs are promises of inner delights and deep visions. They unfold a Divine order which we can reject in adult age, never discovering the interior joys promised in the Word.

By unfolding the inner meaning of these stories, we can find a pattern for our own lives. What is the ideal growth process, with no interfering emotional disorder? Psychologists tell us that many people are emotionally crippled to some degree, but with most of us this does not stop the process of spiritual growth.[9] Our path may be blocked now and then, but with extra effort we can find our way. We can combine the Divine teachings of the Writings with new psychological ideas to enhance our lives and our children's lives. To do this is to combine both 'foundations of truth' the Lord has given us, and so find fullness of life.[10] It is also to discover in our affections the pathway of the golden thread.

Chapter 9
Abram and Childhood

Now the Lord had said to Abram:
"Get out of your country,
And from your birth,
And from your father's house,
To a land that I will show you.
I will make you a great nation;
I will bless you
And make your name great;
And you shall be a blessing" (Genesis 12:1-2).

These and the things which follow occurred historically, as they are written; but the historicals are representative, and each word is significative. By "Abram" in the internal sense is meant the Lord....By "now the Lord had said to Abram," is signified the first mental awareness of all; "get out of your country," signifies the corporeal and worldly things from which He was to recede; "and from your birth," signifies the more exterior corporeal and worldly things; "and from your father's house," signifies the more interior of such things; "to the land that I will show you," signifies the spiritual and celestial things that were to be presented to view (AC 1407).

"I will make you a great nation," signifies the kingdom in the heavens and on the earth; it is said "a great nation," from things celestial and from goods; "I will bless you," signifies the fructification of celestial things and the multiplication of spiritual things; "and make your name great," signifies glory; "and you shall be a blessing," signifies that from the Lord are all things both in general and in particular (AC 1415).

At first the state of an infant is very obscure. Under the protection of the Spirit of God, innocence is everywhere. Innocence is the very inmost essence of all good and is the first quality of human life. Here, at the beginning of life, a golden thread is given that can lead throughout life on earth to the innocence of wisdom that will endure in heaven to eternity.

The departure of Abram, his wife Sarai, and his nephew Lot from Haran for Canaan depicts the process in human life of the gradual emerging from obscurity. "And they departed to go to the land of Canaan. And into the land of Canaan they came."[1] Canaan represents heaven and "celestial things of love."[2] Celestial angels are then with a tiny baby, working gently through innocence to instill the celestial things of love. There is no state more potent in life until we again become as little children after regeneration is complete.

It is said "Jehovah appeared to Abram." Secretly, an infant 'sees' the Lord.[3] Babies feel complete love for their parents, who stand in place of the Lord. This is the inmost of remains, experienced with an intensity and depth almost above consciousness. As the first state in human life, the celestial is the key to all states that follow. Its trinal quality is innocence, love of the Lord and mutual love. "It is the celestial of love not to desire to be one's own, but to belong to all; so that we desire to give others all that is our own: in this consists the essence of celestial love."[4]

Externally, there are all the needs, wants and innocence of infancy. Internally, infants dwell on a mountain of love with the celestial angels. They are above knowledges, above any turmoil, completely trusting. It is a state of love that is scarcely conceivable; the very heart of remains. The Lord is present, seemingly a helpless lamb. He is nevertheless the Lion of the tribe of Judah.

Are Children All Good?

I will bless those who bless you,
And I will curse him who curses you;
And in you all the families of the earth shall be blessed
(Genesis 12:3).

"I will bless those who bless you," signifies all happiness to those who acknowledge the Lord from the heart; "and I will curse him who curses you," signifies unhappiness to those who do not acknowledge Him; "and in you all the families of the earth shall be blessed," signifies that all things true and good are from the Lord (AC 1421).

The Writings teach that when human life began on earth, in the time of the Most Ancient Church in the golden age before the fall, every infant was born good.[5] The feelings and thoughts of those people, the will and understanding, were inseparable. Hypocrisy was impossible; they lived in childlike innocence. Gradually, however, they turned towards loving themselves more than God and passed this tendency on to their children. As this process continued, the will, once innocent, became corrupt. Since these people could only understand what they could love, falsity engulfed the world, this mental deluge being represented by the story of the flood. The flood was not a natural disaster, but a spiritual flood of falsifications. These cut off the life of the fallen peoples of the Most Ancient Church. And there was mercy in this, for if they had had children, those children would have been doomed to hell.

At this point, the Lord separated the human understanding from the fallen will, so that people could learn truths in spite of their corrupted hereditary natures. He gifted the separated understanding with childhood remains, so that from remains truth could be loved and obeyed. Then they could compel themselves to apply the truths to their lives and gradually the Lord could form in them new wills in the separated understanding until they were reborn into confirmed good. This is still how the Lord regenerates us today.

The Lord not only wished to make regeneration possible after the fall, He wanted it to have some deep delights. He gave us special gifts to enable rebirth to take place through a series of delights, as well as through temptation and trial.[6] "Every age has its delights."[7] He placed these gifts in the understanding separated from the fallen will. The inmost of these are the first remains of infancy.

The years of infancy are not all innocence. Unlike the celestial person of the golden age, the spiritual person of our age has inherited evil tendencies. The hells are not allowed to spiritually tempt in infancy or childhood, but they are present through hereditary evil. Because of this, the *Arcana Caelestia* calls evil a "nurse" to the infant.[8] Yet parents and teachers can limit, temper and help subordinate this evil presence.[9]

> I have talked with angels about little children, whether they are free from evils, inasmuch as they have no actual evil as adults have; and I was told that they are equally in evil, and in fact are nothing but evil; but, like all angels, they are so withheld from evil and held in good by the Lord as to seem to themselves to be in good from themselves. For this reason, when children have become adults in heaven, that they may not have the false idea about themselves that the good in them is from themselves and not from the Lord, they are now and then let down into their evils which they inherited, and are left in them until they know, acknowledge and believe the truth of the matter (HH 342).

We cannot be blind to the reality of hereditary evil in children,[10] but it is held in a general subjection so that the Lord can implant remains.[11] "Any one who thinks from any enlightened reason can see that no man is born for hell, for the Lord is love itself, and His love is to will the salvation of all."[12] Even more directly: "Every one who thinks from reason can be sure that all are born for heaven and no one for hell, and if man comes into hell he himself is culpable; but *little children cannot be held culpable.*"[13]

Being aware of remains or innocent childhood affections can shape how we approach children. Viewed from their states of remains they are guiltless. All three degrees of the celestial have innocence within them[14] and are summarized by the word 'guiltlessness.' Little children are in a good state inwardly from remains. Essentially, that is how we are to view them. We should be as the Lord, who "imputes good to every man and evil to none."[15]

Parents can help children maintain their innocence. They have to provide true order for infants, so that they may eventually learn self-discipline. But, discipline should come from love:

> Love introduces order immediately into the understanding . . . .
> Man is successively introduced into order from his infancy . . . . The laws of order are Divine truths . . . . In proportion

as man receives love, in the same proportion he makes order for himself.... Man can get himself into a state of order in proportion as he gets himself into a state of love.... True order is connected with decorum, beauty, elegance, perfection (Add. to TCR, PTW: I, p. 154).

The celestial level is the origin of the genuine love that introduces true and complete order. On the outward plane, children reciprocate with obedience, which keeps hereditary evil in its place.

Education

Now there was a famine in the land, and Abram went down to Egypt to sojourn there... (Genesis 12:10).

How do celestial remains affect later states, aside from being within them? When do these first remains surface to help the growing child and adult? How can the knowledge of remains be used to help in child rearing, in education and throughout the rest of life?

After Abram's first sojourn in the land of Canaan, he journeyed on toward the south. His going into Egypt represents the end of infancy and entrance into childhood and 'formal' education. From inmost love there is a state of light that leads to a real desire to learn.[16] "The famine in the land" is a scarcity of knowledges, the time when children begin to hunger for learning. Sojourning in Egypt represents instruction in knowledges, satisfying the intense childhood wonder and curiosity.

The celestial level ideally guides all succeeding states. The innocence of the celestial does not mean passivity: "the celestial itself cannot possibly exist without activity."[17] Its first activity is worship.[18] By its origin from the Lord, worship is spontaneous with the celestial. The highest educational priority is to help children to have a fulfilling spiritual life centered on loving and worshipping the Lord.

The activity of love is shown not only in worship; it is especially expressed in uses. These are expressions of the originating love shaped by truths and knowledges. Education should foster a use-oriented, creative child. Such a child will find avenues of discovery and expression throughout the educational process, motivated by inner love. The world of imagination, full of growing knowledges, awaits the creative work of a child. This does not preclude necessary study and drill, but looks upon them as a means to the end.

Remains are supportive of genuine use and creativity. A child has imagination and creativity descending from the highest levels. True education allows these to grow and flourish in an atmosphere of true order, meeting children's needs 'head on' by knowledges open to higher levels.[19]

An interesting possible confirmation of this is the implication of a Harvard Preschool Project.[20] It found that children who were imaginative and exploratory had mothers who gave their full attention to their children at critical times, listened to questions in a genuinely caring way, and helped the children find answers as far as possible through their own exploration.

These "A" type mothers treated children as human beings with creative potential and surrounded them with an environment that encouraged that creativity. This was not mayhem or permissiveness; it was an ordered and gently guided opening up to creativity and exploration. The "C" type mothers did not encourage creativity but stressed outward order without inward interest or buoyancy.

The critical ages for establishing life patterns of attitude were found to be from ten months to one and one-half years old, with the suspicion that the real start might be earlier. The researchers were astonished. If nothing else, this tends to support the idea of the great power of early remains as active forces in response to learning.

Basically, education should be *a priori* in approach—from prior things, flowing from what is higher to what is lower:

> ...if you take away that which is interior, the exterior falls; for the exterior comes into existence and subsists from its interiors in order. So it is with innocence. This makes one with love to the Lord (AC 5608).

> ...Something shall be said respecting order. The order is for the celestial to inflow into the spiritual and adapt it to itself; for the spiritual thus to inflow into the rational and thus adapt it to itself, and for the rational thus to inflow into the knowledge and adapt it to itself (see AC 1495:2). But when a man is

being instructed in his earliest childhood, the order is indeed the same, but it appears otherwise, namely, [it appears] that he advances from knowledge to rational things, from these to spiritual things, and so at last to celestial things. The reason it so appears is that a way must be opened to celestial things, which are inmost. All instruction is simply *an opening of the way* [to celestial things] (AC 1495:2; italics added).

Children should be educated in a way that is open to the celestial level—a way that leads to their inner hearts. Their affections should not be cut off by empty knowledges,[21] but allowed to blossom by nurturing creativity. Education can be based on spiritual truths, opening children's thoughts to higher levels instead of just focusing on the earth. If 'open' knowledges are taught with imagination, the celestial is stirred to life and deeply moves the young listener.

When questioned as to the greatest authority, Jesus set a little child "in the midst of them."[22] The celestial, from the remains of infancy, is to be "in the midst" of the entire educational process as the authority.

Children are led from the external innocence in which they are at the beginning and which is called the innocence of childhood, to internal innocence, which is the innocence of wisdom. This innocence is the end that directs all their instruction and progress; and therefore when they have attained to the innocence of wisdom, the innocence of childhood, which in the meanwhile has served them as a plane, is joined to them (HH 341).

This describes a path that does not end with formal education, but continues throughout life.

Chapter 10

Abraham and Adolescence

After these things the word of Jehovah came to Abram in a vision, saying, "Do not be afraid, Abram. I am your shield, your exceedingly great reward...." Then He brought him outside and said, "Look now toward heaven, and count the stars if you are able to number them." And He said to him, "So shall your descendants be" (Genesis 15:1,5).

"After these things the word of Jehovah came to Abram in a vision," signifies that after the combats in childhood there was revelation; "a vision" denotes inmost revelation, which is that of perception; "Do not be afraid, Abram. I am your shield," signifies protection against evils and falsities, which is to be trusted; "your great reward," signifies the end or purpose of the victories (AC 1784).

"He brought him outside," signifies the sight of the interior man which from external things sees internal; "and said, 'Look now toward heaven,' " signifies a representation of the Lord's kingdom in a mental view of the universe; "and count the stars," signifies a representation of things good and true in a mental view of the constellations; "if you are able to number them," signifies the fruitfulness of love and multiplication of faith; "And He said to him, 'So shall your descendants be,' " signifies the heirs of the Lord's kingdom (AC 1805).

The stories of the patriarchs represent not only our own lives, but the life of Jesus. The Writings tell us that He was educated by direct communication with His Divine soul. Jehovah gave Him an intuitive perception of the correspondences of everything in nature to spiritual qualities. His life and education provide an ideal pattern for ours.

Seventh grade (age 12-13) begins the often stormy transition from childhood to adolescence.[1] The wars of Chedorlaomer[2] can picture the rebellions of early adolescence. Like the kings of Sodom and Gomorrah, for "twelve years they served Chedorlaomer, and in the thirteenth year they rebelled."[3] In the thirteenth year they rebelled; this sounds somewhat familiar! These wars are the awakening of a frightening selfishness that is graphically depicted in the people of Sodom and Gomorrah. This rebellious state does come to an end, followed by a time of peace. However, the same selfishness returns later in a more troubling form.

After these first struggles, there is a release from arrogance, a beautiful drawing back from too much merit. Chedorlaomer is conquered by Abram. Then an interior peace descends into the hearts and thoughts of many eighth graders. "And Melchizedek king of Salem brought out bread and wine; he was the priest of God Most High."[4] Melchizedek was one of the few remaining people from the Ancient Church—a symbol of the forgotten celestial and "peace as to interior or rational things."[5] Here at the end of childhood, this vestige of innocence comes to bless the end of the whole state before the passage into adolescence. He brings the wine of spiritual childhood remains and the bread of the celestial remains of infancy.[6] This peace after turmoil can be felt in open discussions with thirteen- and fourteen-year-olds.

Following the final blessing of childhood is the first vision of adolescence. The Lord gives hope and reassurance during the vulnerable time of transition: "Do not be afraid, Abram. I am your shield, your exceedingly great reward."[7] Then He brings Abram out to look at the stars. When Jesus was an adolescent in state, He was also led by His soul into the night to look at the stars. As He gazed at them, a Divine perception inflowed: the number of future angels in heaven would be as immense as the number of stars. He needed this realization because He had just endured a hard spiritual battle, experiencing frightening doubts about whether the human race could be saved. The reassurance by Jehovah that there would be millions upon millions of future angels gave Him a most profound joy.[8]

This vision of the stars portrays for adolescents the first awe-inspiring realization of the operation of the Lord in creation, and the excitement for them of seeing future perceptions spread out ahead. The vision also shows us a new way of seeing earthly things. In viewing the stars, Abram (the Lord as a child) was to see beyond them to all the future angels they represented, and to all future states of good and truth with men and angels. The countless stars depicted these states. From earthly things, Jesus was to see great spiritual truths by correspondences:

> Things internal are led forth, when with the eyes of the body a man contemplates the starry heaven, and thence thinks of the Lord's kingdom. Whenever a man sees anything with his eyes, and sees the things that he looks upon as if he saw them not, but from them thinks of the things which are of the church or of heaven, then his interior sight...is "brought outside" (AC 1806).

> For there is nothing beautiful and delightful in the skies or on the earth, which is not in some way representative of the Lord's kingdom.... This is the "looking toward heaven" which signifies a representation of the Lord's kingdom in a mental view of the universe. The reason why all things in the sky and on earth are representative, is that they have come forth and do continually come forth, that is, subsist, from the influx of the Lord through heaven (AC 1807).

This new paradigm, this vision of Abram, can apply to everyone in the high school years. Jesus was yearning for a Divine explanation of creation and life; this same desire comes to most young people. Within it is the hope for adult vision or rationality. It is a prayer for an explanation of the purposes of God—for an understanding of creation and its meaning, and of the nature and quality of His love.

It would be ideal if a student could be led to:

> ...see internal things from external; that is, that he may, from the objects in the world, reflect continually upon those which are in the other life; for this is the life for the sake of which he lives in the world. Such was the sight in the Most Ancient Church; such is the sight of the angels who are with man; and such was the Lord's sight (AC 1806).

What a beautiful challenge to teachers and students in high school! This is a profoundly poetic yet nevertheless genuine approach to life. All things in nature: the stars, the sunrise, the seasons, oceans, the tiniest cycles within flowers and trees, correspond to spiritual realities and to qualities in the Lord. This is also the heart of true science, since natural laws correspond to spiritual laws, which can be illustrated in chemistry, physics, in the nature of the human body, in biology and cell life and in mathematics. The vision of Abram could be applied implicitly or explicitly throughout secondary education, making learning also spiritual instead of only natural: "Seek first the kingdom of God and His righteousness."[9]

This may sound too idealistic, too abstract and remote. What relation has all this in the *Arcana Caelestia* to the lively, cynical, sometimes crude, sometimes delightful adolescents we know? The Writings deal with the inner goals, the leading principles which must govern if there is to be any spiritual success or true education. This vision of heavenly things from earthly things can only come *a priori*—only if the celestial is inflowing strongly into the present lower state. All true perception comes from the celestial plane. The adolescent can be open to this vision if there is compassion and true order in the approach of the teacher or parent.

"A Terror of Great Darkness"

Now when the sun was going down, a deep sleep fell upon Abram; and behold, a terror of great darkness fell upon him (Genesis 15:12).

"The sun was going down," signifies the time and the state before the consummation . . . . A "deep sleep," relatively to one of wakefulness, denotes a dark state . . . . That "a terror of great darkness fell upon him," means that the Lord was horrified at so great a vastation. So far as any one is in the celestial things of love, so far does he feel horror when he perceives a consummation (AC 1836-1839).

After the vision of the stars, after truly seeing something of the Lord in creation and in life, the insight begins to fall away. Adolescents see, for the first time, something of the nature of hereditary evil in themselves which waits to attack openly in adult life. This is a devastating realization; childhood innocence is threatened with loss. The inner heart feels horror. The Lord Himself, when as a child He first saw the nature of human evil, wished to withdraw from the perception. The nature of that evil "struck Him with horror."[10]

There is a powerful need for reassurance, for affection and guidance. Jehovah promised Abram that all would eventually be well; there would be a time of enslavement but freedom from evil would come.[11] In the world, this horror is the time when 'adult' evils can hit and undermine a young person's life: addiction to drugs or alcohol, sexual misuse, cruelties and hatred. Our education should deal not only with the head, but far more compassionately with the emotions and heart. Adolescents need deep emotional reassurance.

The Covenant

And I give to you and your descendants after you the land in which you are a stranger, all the land of Canaan, as an everlasting possession; and I will be their·God (Genesis 17:7-8).

The covenant between Jehovah and Abram is critical in our lives. Coming at the end of adolescence, it is a nexus between the remains of childhood and the adventure of adult life. The stirring of conjugial hope comes from the celestial plane flowing into the minds of the adolescents. Through conjugial love, which is "celestial, spiritual, holy, pure and clean above every love,"[12] God conjoins Himself to us.

Jehovah commands circumcision for Abram and his male children. This corresponds to the removal of those things which defile celestial love.[13] There is a time in adolescence when nothing is sweeter than the promise of falling in love. This is the bridge from childhood to adult life. The adolescent's part in the covenant is to circumcise the heart—to shun what opposes conjugial love. This means looking to the Lord in prayer for help and then actively shunning lust and sexual abuse. Even with failures, this shunning in intention and act ushers in true rationality with an idealism that is genuine, not counterfeit nor sentimental. This idealism is the basis for all future spiritual growth.

As part of the covenant, Jehovah changes Abram's name to Abraham. In Jesus' life, this represents putting off His human qualities, and taking on the Divine.[14] With Abram, "because he was to represent the Lord, and in fact His internal man, and thus the celestial of His love, his former quality was to be blotted out...."[15]

After facing the adult reality of the 'great darkness,' adolescents change in quality.

> ...The name "Abram" was to be so changed in character that the Lord could be represented by it. Therefore the letter H was taken from the name of Jehovah—which letter is the only one in the name "Jehovah" that involves the Divine, and which signifies I AM, or BEING *(Esse)*—and was inserted in his name, and he was called "Abraham" (AC 2010).

"Who am I?" becomes an important question for adolescents in the stage psychologist Erik Erikson calls "identity versus identity confusion."[16] The old childhood self is overwhelmed by the tide of new feeling and thoughts. Adult spiritual life is on the horizon, with new freedom and rationality. The question of 'which self?' is felt acutely as it arises for the first time. The array of possible selves is bewildering! It is comforting to know that deep within is our spiritual identity inscribed on the childhood self, and that this can lead back to innocence.

The celestial remains of infancy can still flow into the lower states that follow:

> ...In the external man all is natural....The internal man is said to be united to the external when the celestial spiritual of the internal man flows into the natural of the external, and makes them act as one. As a consequence of this, the natural also becomes celestial and spiritual, but a lower celestial and spiritual...(AC 1577:3).

The Lord gives us the covenant that, even though childhood is over, later in life we can return to the land of celestial love. The golden thread leads the way.

Chapter 11

Ishmael: The Birth of Reason

And the Angel of Jehovah said to her:
"Behold, you are with child,
And you shall bear a son.
You shall call his name Ishmael,
Because Jehovah has heard your affliction."

"He shall be a wild-ass man;
His hand shall be against all,
And the hand of all against him.
And he shall dwell against the faces of all his brethren"
(Genesis 16:11-12).

"The angel of Jehovah said to her," signifies the thought of
the interior man; "Behold, you are with child," signifies the
life of the rational man; "and you shall bear a son," signifies
the truth of the same; "you shall call his name Ishmael,"
signifies the state of its life; "because Jehovah has heard your
affliction," signifies while it was submitting itself (AC 1942).

"He shall be a wild-ass man," signifies rational truth, which
is described; "his hand shall be against all," signifies that it
will wage war upon whatever is not true, "and the hand of all
against him," signifies that falsities will fight back; "and he
shall dwell against the faces of all his brethren," signifies that
there will be continual contentions about matters of faith; but
that nevertheless it will be a conqueror (AC 1948).

About thirteen years before the covenant that changed
Abram's name to Abraham, his wife Sarai, unable herself to
conceive, gave him her Egyptian maid Hagar so that they could
have a child. Abram was about eighty-six and he and Sarai were
childless. As soon as Hagar conceived, she began to hate Sarai.
With Abram's permission, Sarai "dealt harshly with her."[1]
Hagar fled into the wilderness, where the Angel of Jehovah

appeared and told her to return and said, "I will multiply your descendants exceedingly, so that they shall not be counted for multitude."[2]

Hagar represents "the life of the exterior or natural man"[3] and, as an Egyptian handmaid, "the affection of scientifics."[4] The role she represents in our childhood is the mother of the first form of rationality that leads. to the adult frame of mind.

Ishmael is born before the covenant, before the human in the Lord was made Divine, and with us before our quality changes. He represents the reasoning power and love of reasoning that comes in adolescence. The wild-ass "signifies man's rational; not, however, the rational in its whole complex, but only rational truth. The rational consists of good and truth."[5] Ishmael is the cold, hard intellect with no softening love, reasoning from the senses alone.

> It seems incredible that rational truth when separated from good should be of such a character....The man whose rational is of such a character that he is solely in truth—even though it be the truth of faith—and who is not at the same time in the good of charity, is altogether of such a character. He is a morose man, will bear nothing, is against all, regards everybody as being in falsity, is ready to rebuke, to chastise, and to punish; has no pity, and does not apply or adapt himself to others or study to bend their minds; for he looks at everything from truth, and at nothing from good (AC 1949).

Even though Ishmael is wild and rebellious, Abram loves him. In the covenant, Jehovah says: "And as for Ishmael, I have heard you. Behold, I have blessed him, and will make him fruitful, and will multiply him exceedingly. He shall beget twelve princes, and I will make him a great nation."[6] The reasoning faculty can be fruitful when it is not placed as the highest of the mind's abilities.

Isaac Is Born

> For Sarah conceived and bore Abraham a son in his old age....So the child grew and was weaned. And Abraham made a great feast on the same day that Isaac was weaned. And Sarah saw the son of Hagar the Egyptian, whom she had

borne to Abraham, scoffing. Therefore she said to Abraham, "Cast out this bondwoman and her son; for the son of this bondwoman shall not be heir with my son, namely with Isaac" (Genesis 21:2,8-10).

"...For the son of this bondwoman shall not be heir with my son, namely with Isaac," signifies that the merely human rational could not have a common life with the Divine rational itself, either as to truth or as to good (AC 2655).

Spiritual rationality is represented by Abraham's son Isaac, born after the covenant to Sarah (Sarai). Sarah is "truth adjoined to good.[7] The Ishmael form of rationality arises "through ... the senses;"[8] it sees in the light of the world. The Isaac rational is "formed by the Lord through the affection of spiritual truth and good,"[9] and sees in the light of heaven. Ishmael *reasons* from his senses; Isaac *perceives* spiritual truths.

There are ... two principles, one of which leads to all folly and insanity, and the other to all intelligence and wisdom. The former principle is to deny all things, or to say in the heart that we cannot believe them until we are convinced by what we can apprehend or perceive *by the senses*; this is the principle that leads to all folly and insanity, and is to be called the negative principle. The other principle is to affirm the things which are of doctrine from the Word, or to think and believe within ourselves that they are true because the Lord has said them; this is the principle that leads to all intelligence and wisdom, and is to be called the affirmative principle (AC 2568; italics added).

We cannot prove a single spiritual truth with reason alone. There are successive planes of the human mind, one above the other: sensation, imagination, reason and perception—spiritual perception. Each can see on its own plane, but cannot see into the planes above it. Divine revelation is addressed to the highest conscious plane of the human mind on earth—the plane of perception. Perception is our *spiritual* sensation, enabling us to see clearly that revealed rational truth is true.

This spiritual vision of truth is convincing beyond doubt and superior to that of the lower plane of reason. The Writings are a rational Divine revelation; perception sees that they are true.

Still, revelation is not unreasonable; the Writings speak to the reason when it is under subordination to the higher quality of perception. We are invited to "enter intellectually into the mysteries of faith."[10]

Ishmael Today

Woe to those who are wise in their own eyes, and intelligent before their own faces (Is. 5:21).

They are called "drunkards" [in the Word] who believe nothing but what they apprehend, and for this reason search into the mysteries of faith . . . . Indeed, the souls or spirits who in the other life reason about the truths of faith and against them become like drunken man and act like them (AC 1072).

There is a saying in the Virgin Islands: "try to be too wise, you end up otherwise." We see the wisdom of these words in the world around us. Technology is threatening to annihilate the planet, either with a bang or a slowly poisoned whimper. 'Wisdom' separated from love creates a cold, hard environment in spite of its 'miracles.'

The approach of many in the intellectual world is not from spiritual perception. Sense-oriented reasoning has established a causeless evolution working through the laws of natural selection as the basis of life. Just how the first life arose is a mystery, but from there on some evolutionists, through a marvelous series of facts unfortunately viewed backwards, have ushered God out of creation. Revelation is dismissed by many intellectuals as a human invention—a wish-creation in the naive struggle to find an eternal life and a God. If reason rejects subordination to heavenly perception, the 'negative principle' dominates. Yet creation speaks of a Creator!

The negative principle has infiltrated the modern world. The process began centuries ago. It goes back at least to the sixteenth century, when Francis Bacon introduced the 'inductive method' of discovering truth. Over the centuries, this has been refined into the 'scientific method.' Its approach is *a posteriori*; that is, through induction, in which effects are analyzed to arrive at causes. Used correctly, the scientific method is *not* the negative principle, but if it is made a god and turned towards the heavens, then it becomes Ishmael perverted.

The abuse of the rational comes in the endeavor to analyze a discretely higher plane from one below it. The attempt has been made to do the impossible—to discover *spiritual* causes from natural effects. "No one can apprehend higher things from lower ones, that is, spiritual and celestial, still less Divine things from lower ones, because they transcend all [lower] understanding."[11] "The prior, because in itself it is purer, cannot appear to the posterior because in itself it is grosser."[12]

> From effects nothing but effects can be learned. When effects alone are considered, no causes are brought to light. But causes reveal effects. To know effects from causes is to be wise; but to search out causes from effects is not to be wise, because fallacies then present themselves, which the investigator calls causes, and this is to turn wisdom into foolishness. Causes are things prior, and effects are things posterior; and things prior cannot be seen from things posterior, but things posterior can be seen from things prior. This is order. For this reason the spiritual world is here first treated of, for all causes are there; and afterwards the natural world, where all things that appear are effects (DLW 119).

Objective scientists and seekers of truth recognize the error of abusing induction. They reject unproved assertions concerning spiritual causes. Francis Bacon himself, in *Novum Organum*, states: "Man, as the minister and interpreter of nature, does and understands as much as his observation on the order of nature . . . permits him; and neither knows nor is capable of more."[13]

But his successors applied the inductive method to realms in which it has no place, using it to explain God, the Word and spiritual causes. Gradually, human reason itself was made God and it was believed that all our knowledge comes through experience and through the senses.

The truth is that spiritual truth is perceived in revelation and then confirmed by reason. Creation is to be viewed in Divine light—*a priori*—from above. Then reason and experience can assume their proper roles, and the world of our lower mind is flooded with the light of heaven. This submission of a lower plane to the one above it leads to seeing the heavenly order which can rule our minds. "The order is for the celestial to inflow into the spiritual and adapt it to itself; for the spiritual thus to flow into the rational and adapt it to itself; and for the rational thus to inflow into...knowledge and adapt it to itself."[14] Ishmael is subordinated and Isaac is the heir. The rational mind becomes whole.

"A Great Nation"

And the Lord will strike Egypt, He will strike and heal it; they will return to the Lord, and He will be entreated by them and heal them. In that day there will be a highway from Egypt to Assyria, and the Assyrian will come into Egypt and the Egyptian into Assyria, and the Egyptians will serve with the Assyrians. In that day Israel will be one of the three with Egypt and Assyria, even a blessing in the midst of the land, whom the Lord of hosts shall bless, saying, "Blessed is Egypt My people, and Assyria the work of My hands, and Israel My inheritance" (Isaiah:19:22-25).

In the spiritual sense this means that at the time of the Lord's coming the scientific, the rational and the spiritual will make one, and that the scientific will then serve the rational, and both the spiritual; for,..."Egypt" signifies the scientific, "Assyria" the rational, and "Israel" the spiritual (TCR 200:4).

Does the inductive method have a legitimate place, or is Ishmael to be cast out forever? Hagar and Ishmael were dying of thirst in the wilderness when the angel of Jehovah told her to "Arise, lift up the lad and hold him with your hand, for I will make him a great nation."[15] Ishmael as a rebel, a mocker, represents the perverted natural rational. But once the proper series of influx from the celestial down through to the sensual is established, he is no longer a traitor to heaven. The natural rational still exists, but is now subservient to the spiritual rational.

Ishmael becomes a "great nation," or the "spiritual church, which will receive the good of faith."[16] The rational and the scientific flow naturally and abundantly from the spiritual plane when they are properly aligned with it. Then inductive reasoning can perform a host of uses for the human mind.

Induction is highly useful as long as it does not try to break through the barrier of discrete degrees:

The interiors which are not open to view can in no way be discovered except through a knowledge of degrees. For things exterior advance to things interior and through these to things inmost, by means of degrees; not by continuous degrees but by discrete degrees. "Continuous degrees" is a term applied to the gradual lessenings or decreasings from grosser to finer, or from denser to rarer; or rather, to growths and increasings from finer to grosser, or from rarer to denser; precisely like the gradations of light to shade, or of heat to cold. But discrete degrees are entirely different: they are like things prior, subsequent and final; or like end, cause, and effect. These degrees are called discrete, because the prior is by itself, the subsequent by itself, and the final by itself; and yet taken together they make one (DLW 184).

On each separate plane or degree there are ends, causes, and effects. It is possible to study the effects of one plane and to induce from these the laws, the causes and ends, of that same plane. Then induction can work wonders, such as the scientific and technological accomplishments of modern civilization.

In view of what this scientific method has accomplished, it is no wonder that pride has made a false god out of it. Trying to raise up a tower of Babel through scientific reasoning to break through to God is understandable. Our culture's pride in scientific and technological miracles has made us easy prey for the serpent's tantalizing promise: "the day you eat of [the tree] your eyes will be opened, and you will be like gods, knowing good and evil."[17]

Abuse does not condemn proper use. Induction is an important part of living faith. In studying revelation, unbiased reason is used to read and reflect upon it first, and then the Lord can inflow into this with heavenly perception. Induction precedes perception; Ishmael precedes Isaac. The water was poured into the vessels at the wedding in Cana before it was miraculously made into wine. Knowledges of a rational revelation are only as water, until the Lord turns the water into wine or the perception of truth.

Perception of truth needs the foundation of reason and science beneath it to be full and truly wise. Inductive reasoning enables us to see *how* a thing is true. It makes it possible for heavenly perception to inflow into and through reason, to flow down even into the scientifics of this world. It brings heavenly light to earth.

> They who think from an affirmative principle can confirm themselves by whatever things rational, by whatever knowledges and whatever things philosophic they have at command; for all these are to them things confirmatory and give them a fuller idea of the matter (AC 2568).

> To become intelligent, a wise man must learn many things, both things pertaining to heaven and things pertaining to the world: things pertaining to heaven from the Word and from the church, and things pertaining to the world from the sciences . . . . The simple are those whose interiors have been opened, but not so enriched by spiritual, moral, civil and natural truths. But the wise . . . are those whose interiors have been both opened and enriched . . . . All this makes clear what true intelligence is and what true wisdom is (HH 351).

Induction has made some people think that God is dead. But we need not feel too superior. It can darken parts of our minds at times and make us feel as if God were dead. False induction, if carried into life, can crucify the Lord for us.

If we can order our minds, putting the perception of His reality first, then the weapon that was destroying—induction—can become a sword of truth. Induction is held in its place and light can inflow into all the corners of the mind. The Lord is brought to life in the lower planes of the mind, where He was believed to be dead. For the Divine is omnipresent in creation. Induction as the servant of perception can enable us to see Him on every plane of science and life. For He is not dead, "He is risen, as He said."[18]

> . . . In respect to those that have acquired intelligence and wisdom through knowledge and science, who are such as have applied all things to the use of life, and have also acknowledged the Divine, loved the Word, and lived a spiritual moral life . . . , to such the sciences have served as a means of becoming wise, and also of corroborating the things pertaining to faith. The interiors of the mind of such have been

perceived by me, and were seen as transparent from light of a glistening white, flamy, or blue color, like that of translucent diamonds, rubies and sapphires; and this in accordance with confirmations in favor of the Divine and Divine truths drawn from science. Such is the appearance of true intelligence and wisdom when they are presented to view in the spiritual world (HH 356).

Chapter 12

The Covenant with Isaac

Then God said: "Truly, Sarah your wife shall bear you a son,
and you shall call his name Isaac; I will establish My covenant with him for an everlasting covenant, and with his
descendants after him" (Genesis 17:19).

Isaac's birth was a miracle. The Lord promised Abraham and
Sarah that it would happen, and they both laughed![1] Abraham
was a hundred years old and Sarah was ninety; she "had passed
the age of childbearing."[2] When Isaac was born, Sarah said,
"God has made me laugh, so that all who hear will laugh with
me."[3] Her laugh of disbelief had been replaced by one of
joy—"the affection of celestial truth."[4]

Isaac was named from "laughter."[5] This is completely different from the mocking laughter of Ishmael, since the origin of
Isaac is Abraham and Sarah, celestial love and inmost truth.
"The origin and essence of laughter...is...the affection of
truth...from which comes the gladness and merriment that in
laughter display themselves in the face."[6] This innocent laughter has its origin in remains and it is simply sheer joy at spiritual
reality.[7]

Isaac represents the spiritual rational that is able to perceive
revelation as true. It is this rational that the Lord is addressing in
the Writings. In youth, this first perceptive rational is in its
infancy, like Isaac at birth. Ishmael is older and stronger; the
rebellious adolescent rational mocks first tender recognitions of
'ethereal' truths. The Ishmael rational has to be cast out so that
the fledgling quality can grow unhampered; its innocence cannot live in mockery.

Rational truth can only be perceived as Divine from innocent celestial love, that love in us that completely trusts the Lord. The lower reason of the spiritual man (Ishmael) cannot believe it to be true.[8]

Isaac depicts the beginning of spiritual adulthood; his growth represents the development of faith. For the first time, the faculties of freedom and genuine rationality are blossoming. We take responsibility for our own lives, natural and spiritual. Once a sure rational faith has been established and can stand freely on its own feet, then we are fully ready for the sweet gift of falling in love and true marriage, and for inner uses that were unknown before.

Falling in Love and Betrothal

Now Abraham was old, well advanced in age.... Abraham said to the oldest servant of his house ... "you shall go to my country and to my kindred, and take a wife for my son Isaac.... The Lord ... shall send His angel before you" (Genesis 24:1,2,4,7).

"And take a wife for my son Isaac," signifies that thence was the affection of truth which should be conjoined with the affection of good of the rational...." He shall send His angel before you," signifies the Divine providence (AC 3022, 3034).

The servant traveled to Mesopotamia, to the city of Nahor. Rebekah came out to the well of water at evening time, and the Lord revealed to the servant that this was to be Isaac's wife. When the servant told his story, Laban and Bethuel— Rebekah's closest relatives—said: "The thing comes from the Lord."[9] Rebekah herself chose to consent, to follow the servant freely. She met Isaac in Canaan in a field at eventide and in time they fell most deeply in love.

The Lord sending His angel represents the Divine providence leading with special power toward love truly conjugial— the eternal union of souls in marriage. This gift from the Lord is written on our inmost souls, above our consciousness. His angel comes secretly when we open the way to innocence and the celestial. This is the source of 'falling in love' as if by chance.

Of course, there are times when it is not the 'real thing.' It is fairly common to 'fall in love with love,' innocently but unrealistically romanticizing the conjugial ideal. A person can become enchanted by beauty, sex, wealth, or someone who is just not 'the right person,' and can pour all the power of the most profound remains into a relationship.

It is also not unusual to try to fill a desperate emotional vacuum with a love relationship. The unsatisfied need for a loving father or mother can be transferred to a symbiotic relationship with a surrogate willing to fit the role. There can be real love above the symbiosis, but this is terribly dangerous territory. It is better to be a full adult, emotionally and spiritually, before embarking on the adventure of marriage. Otherwise the marriage can be pathetically unhappy.

A person's own spiritual and emotional identity needs to be strong before it is possible to have the flexibility to be in a full giving and receiving relationship, before there can be a full conjugial relationship. Erik Erikson calls this stage of life 'intimacy versus isolation,' which comes after 'identity versus identity confusion':

> It is only when identity formation is well on its way that true intimacy—which is really a counterpointing as well as a fusing of identities —is possible. Sexual intimacy is only part of what I have in mind, for it is obvious that sexual intimacies often precede the capacity to develop a true and mutual psychosocial intimacy with another person (*Identity, Youth and Crisis*, p. 135).

Erikson believed the stages of life he found were universal. 'Intimacy versus isolation' comes after the confusion of late adolescence. Once we have discovered who we are, we can begin to explore ourselves and others, to reach out. This blossoms fully in conjugial love.

If we 'wait for the Lord' and shun wrong motives, He will send His angel. This is His promise of conjugial love. When it comes, it is touched with the innocence and golden love of celestial remains. Our whole self feels at home with the loved one and we are most deeply touched to think of spending our lives growing together.

127

'Consent' is a quiet word, with the lyrical connotation of being in love. It is followed by the time of betrothal—a state and ceremony that expresses and deepens the union of minds and hearts before the full union of bodies with marriage:

> I will betroth you to Me forever;
> Yes, I will betroth you to Me
> In righteousness and justice,
> In lovingkindness and mercy;
> I will betroth you to Me in faithfulness
> And you shall know the Lord (Hosea 2:19-20).

Conjugial love is profound inner friendship. The essence of the celestial is loving another more than self, and conjugial love is celestial in nature;[10] the golden thread is entwined in it.

> ...It ascends progressively upwards from its first heat towards the souls, with an effort to conjunction there, and this by openings of the minds, continually more interior; and there is no love that more intensely labors for these openings, or which more powerfully and easily opens the interiors of the minds than conjugial love, for the soul of each intends it. But at the same moments when that love is ascending towards the soul, it is descending also towards the body, and is thereby clothing itself. But it should be known that conjugial love is of such quality in its descent as it is in the altitude to which it ascends; if it is in the height, it descends chaste, and if not in the height, it descends unchaste (CL 302).

In the order provided by the Lord, the betrothed couple are virgins because this is the most beautiful way to establish an inner friendship that is not selfish or sensuous. Close love and friendship are shown without sexual intercourse; a kiss or a touch can express tender feelings without the intent to arouse. Virginity is also a state of mind—our thoughts "ought to be raised out of the lowest region into the higher region."[11] This approach brings the Lord's springtime to betrothal, lifting it into a friendship that lasts forever. Virginity expresses the innocence of the golden thread.

For those who are not virgins, by looking upward to the Lord "this lowest region is purified of its unchastities."[12] Sex before marriage and living together endanger the conjugial.[13] How-

129

ever, if we look towards marriage and the Lord, He can bring the conjugial into a relationship that has been on a lower level only. The friendship of love, the marriage of souls, can be opened up and established by refraining from what opposes conjugial love.[14]

This call to chastity is not a trumpet of judgment. In the Book of Revelation, before the trumpets were blown, "another angel, having a golden censer, came and stood at the altar."[15] The angel with the golden censer is perception ascending to the very celestial, the inmost origin of tenderness and astonishingly moving affection. The censer is the conjunction of celestial and spiritual good.[16] Gold is celestial. The trumpet is the Divine truth to be revealed,[17] calling to protect the innocence of conjugial love.

If the innocence of the golden thread enters betrothal, the future marriage is truly full of the whole ladder of ascending and descending loves. Then the ultimate of physical union after the wedding is not just powerful on its own level, but expresses the magic of love on inner levels (betrothal loves). All of the planes can be together then in the ultimate, renewed because of the wonder of the loves within. Springtime and the marriage of minds has preceded; now is the summer of full love. It should be added that sexual knowledge is not innate, and it is proper for instruction in loving sexual intercourse to be taken by the husband (and perhaps his future wife) just before marriage. A full loving sexual relationship in marriage is only gradually learned, and calls for patience and tenderness. But the full inner and outer joy is there, waiting to be found and developed to eternity.

Betrothal is springtime; the seeds of a fruitful, abundant relationship flower within. This is not just natural romance, full of temporary illusions. Real falling in love is a fulfilling, celestial gift from the Lord. Betrothal functions on the highest level to establish the eternal in marriage.

Marriage

Then Isaac brought her into his mother Sarah's tent; and he took Rebekah and she became his woman, and he loved her. So Isaac was comforted after his mother's death (Gen 24:67).

"Then Isaac brought her into his mother Sarah's tent," signifies the sanctuary of truth in the Divine Human (AC 3208). "And he took Rebekah and she became his woman, and he loved her,"...signifies the conjunction...of good and truth (AC 3211). "So Isaac was comforted after his mother's death,"...signifies a new state...of glorification of the rational; as before in respect to good, so now in respect to truth...when man is being regenerated, he is then becoming altogether another, and is being made new; therefore also when he has been regenerated, he is called "born again," and "created anew." Then, although he has a similar face and a similar speech, yet his mind is not similar; his mind, when he is regenerate, is open toward heaven, and there dwells in love to the Lord and charity toward his neighbor, together with faith. It is the mind that makes a man another, and a new man (AC 3212).

The more fully we love the Lord, the more fully we receive conjugial love, which can come interiorly with or without a partner on earth. The process of rebirth is the marriage of good and truth within us, a coming to wholeness and fruition. Our inner and outer natures join in harmony, and the love and wisdom we receive from God pour out to others. This is expressed in true marriage love.

"In the image of God He created him; male and female He created them."[18] A man ideally is love veiled over with wisdom, and a woman wisdom veiled over with love.[19] Outwardly, the male is the image of understanding and judgment, and the female the likeness of love and intuition. He is the lungs and she is the heart. Together they form the "image and likeness of God."[20] When their souls and minds are joined they inwardly become one. In heaven, they are seen from a distance as one angel! Their natures, equal and complementary, balance each other delightfully.

On earth, married partners can help each other to grow spiritually. Often, the woman helps the man to get out of his 'male ego' conceit; and the man can balance the woman's tendency to view things emotionally. Within, she has the wisdom of understanding his nature, and he has his love for her. She is the recipient of conjugial love; he feels it from her. Ideally he comes into the light of truth, which she receives from him. As they regenerate together, her will becomes their will and his understanding becomes their understanding.

Once love for each other is growing, it flows out to others. "In the highest region, called celestial, is conjugial chastity in its love; into this man is raised by the love of uses; and as the most excellent uses are from marriages, into this celestial region man is raised by love truly conjugial."[21] We are raised up by conjugial love because it "powerfully and easily opens the interiors of the minds."[22] When we are so opened to the Lord, we love our neighbors and love to perform uses for them.

True conjugial love is "effected by uses and according to them, which uses both [husband and wife] by mutual aid perform in society."[23] Angelic couples work together to help those around them. Because their natures complement each other, together they have a balanced, whole perspective. This idea has exciting possibilities which we have hardly begun to touch upon here on earth.

The uses of conjugial love begin in the home, where love and wisdom are most intimately and spontaneously expressed. In heaven, the truths from the man are conceived, carried and brought forth by the woman.[24] "The love of infants corresponds to the protecting of truth and good."[25] Angels do not give birth to children, yet spiritual births—births of new uses, are as tangible and delightful to them as children are to us. It is their fountain of uses, which serves the Grand Man.

We also have spiritual offspring on earth; this is actually the inner origin of our natural children.[26] Children are potential angels, and rearing them is one of the highest uses of conjugial love. Love of having natural children is the ultimate of the love of having spiritual children. Conjugial love, spiritual storgé, and mutual love of others connect with each other in a series,[27] one flowing from the other inseparably.

The Lord's love is the salvation of the human race.[28] Each conjugial couple, in their own way, can serve this same love and use for the Lord. They serve in natural forms on earth and in spiritual forms in heaven—forever! From the home, the uses of conjugial love branch out to human society, and also form the basis of heaven:

... Into conjugial love are gathered all joys and all delights from their first to their last.... Because as already shown conjugial love is the fundamental of all good loves and is inscribed upon the very least parts of man, it follows that its delights exceed the delights of all other loves, and also that it makes all other loves delightful according to its presence and at the same time its conjunction with them. That all delights from their first to their last are gathered into this love, is because of the excellence of its use above all other uses (CL 68).

"A Well of Springing Water"

Then Isaac sowed in that land, and reaped in the same year a hundredfold; and Jehovah blessed him.... And Isaac returned, and dug again the wells of water which they had dug in the days of Abraham his father, for the Philistines had stopped them up after the death of Abraham.... Also Isaac's servants dug in the valley, and found a well of springing water there (Genesis 26:12,18,19).

Isaac's lifetime, as it unfolds, is one of vision, of taking in truth fully and deeply. So often in the literal story he camps by wells of water, because the spiritual rational loves the living waters of Divine truth. Divine truths are also the wells open in childhood, full of "living water ... springing up into everlasting life,"[29] but closed later by adult conceit. Now they are reopened; waters of truth again give full life! But now they are drawn from a fuller, more healing level.

Isaac's life takes us through the beginning of adulthood, falling in love and discovering increasing faith and truths. It is interesting that along with the stage Erikson calls 'intimacy versus isolation' comes a new sense of adult life:

But as the areas of adult responsibility are gradually delineated, ... they eventually become subject to that *ethical sense* which is the mark of the adult and which takes over from the ideological conviction of adolescence and the moralism of childhood (*Identity, Youth & Crisis*, p.136).

This ethical sense comes from the ability to be rational and perceptive.

After the Isaac spiritual rational has been opened, it must be used for spiritual growth. The level of the mind lower than the rational is the natural, and below this is the sensual; these also need to be heaven-made or reborn. So the time comes for a passage away from the rational focus of life into the more practical and applied area of religion: "And it came to pass... Isaac was old, and his eyes were so dim that he could not see."[30] Rational faith begins to lose its vision. To regain clear insight, the natural must now be reborn.

Chapter 13

Jacob's Blessing

May God Shaddai bless you,
And make you fruitful and multiply you,
That you may be an assembly of peoples;
And give you the blessing of Abraham,
To you and your descendants with you,
That you may inherit the land
In which you are a stranger,
Which God gave to Abraham (Genesis 28:3-4).

..."And give you the blessing of Abraham," signifies the conjunction of the Divine Itself with the good and truth of the natural (AC 3666).

With spiritual growth, our focus shifts from inner idealism to day-to-day living. We desire to live our ideals in our home, at work, in the daily challenges of earthly life. Rational vision has grown weak; Isaac, now an old man, looks to his twin sons, Esau and Jacob, to carry on.

Esau corresponds to spontaneous good in the natural, that we yearn to have inflow and govern our work, home and marriage.[1] We want to have this Esau quality come to rule within us, as Isaac wanted to have Esau rule since he was the older son. Who doesn't want good to come easily into natural life? It did in Most Ancient times and it will again when the human race is gradually reborn. But in the meantime, the spiritual person cannot be reborn so easily. We may try to bring good into all things of natural living, but it is hard to do so.

Love for Esau is seen in those who hope to find heaven on earth spontaneously, by living in the order of creation and God—people like Rousseau, Thoreau and some of the existentialists. If we try this method, we see after a time that it breaks down. Something is wrong; in fact, hereditary evil in the natural stands in the way. This evil undermines spontaneous good, so that gradually and even sadly, we see that Jacob must come first for a time.[2]

Jacob represents obeying truth out of self-compulsion, the conscience that comes from following the Divine commandments. Through trial and error, we can finally perceive that we must compel ourselves if our natural plane is to be reborn from the Lord. This is the only route to heaven since the fall of mankind: "If you love Me, *keep My commandments*".[3] In itself, this is not the ideal order, which is shown in the way Jacob deprives Esau out of his birthright and his blessing.[4]

Why do we inherit this heavy burden of evil through no fault of our own? Isn't it an injustice that we are so cursed? How did it happen that others, the Most Ancients, were privileged to receive a good heredity by birth while we suffer? These questions are tormenting when our evils or evil tendencies throw us into unhappiness. One answer is that despite our heredity, we can experience basic happiness throughout our lives, if we follow the path the Lord lays out, even though there are times of temporary sorrow. Regeneration is not as difficult as many believe. Inevitably, in rebirth there are times of deep temptation, but these are means to deeper happiness.

Jacob runs for his life from Esau, fleeing towards Padanaram, his mother's homeland. At the end of a long day's journey, he lies down to sleep, using a stone as a pillow. He dreams of a ladder to heaven and the angels ascending and descending upon it with the Lord standing above. In the dream, the Lord promises that Jacob will eventually return home and will be given the land of Canaan, and that his posterity will be numberless. The dream of the ladder symbolizes an uplifting to the Lord, a time of illustration, vision and hope. At the beginning of a new state, the Lord gives a gift—an ascent into an inspired and heavenly state to prepare for what follows. Like the vision of the stars seen by Abraham, Jacob's dream begins a whole new way of life.

136

Jacob and Laban

Then it came to pass, when Laban heard the report about Jacob his sister's son, that he ran to meet him, and embraced him and kissed him, and brought him to his house (Genesis 29:13).

The ideal progress of regeneration is pictured in the relationship of Laban and Jacob, from their first meeting to their final separation. Their story shows how spiritual contentment may accompany every state of earthly life, except in the despair of temptation. And even such despair can lead to a higher good and happiness.

Jacob travels to Padan-aram and finds Laban and his daughters, Rachel and Leah. Laban represents mediate good, the 'intermediate self' which has both selfishness and innocence within it. A vast part of our hereditary evil is completely hidden from us, protecting us from conscious knowledge of the worst within us. Laban and Jacob are friends for many years; Jacob marries Laban's two daughters. Many of the things we do stem from selfish motives, yet in our own eyes we are acting from worthwhile qualities. Our conscience makes a close friend of our hidden faults, just as Jacob and Laban live and work together. Mediate good includes hidden evil cloaked with real innocence.

We cannot see this hidden evil in ourselves, but we seem to see it in others. We see them doing things that are obviously selfish, but still seem right to them. Our judgment, of course, is based only upon appearances. If we are correct—and that is unknown—then we are seeing the Laban quality in others, evils in them to which they themselves are blind. In fact, in their own consciences they see only good in these selfish qualities.

One powerful lesson we can draw from Jacob and Laban's relationship is that it is against Divine order to criticize others for their evils. Unless they are truly harming other people or uses, we should not speak out, since we also have evils of which we are not aware. If we criticize others before they have the strength to change, we may do them real harm. Only the Lord knows when they are ready. Charity requires us to leave others in freedom to discover and fight their own evils. Respect for this freedom is the highest manifestation of charity and the most difficult, for we have to maintain silence when we see faults we would like to correct. When the time is right, the Lord will open their eyes.

Why are our worst evils hidden from us—why is there this Jacob-Laban relationship in our hearts? This is how the Lord makes it possible for regeneration to be not too difficult.[5] We are unaware of much of our hereditary evils so that they can bring us no deep unhappiness. Since we inherit these evils and are not to blame for them, the Lord does not allow them to destroy our lives. He carefully balances our states so that we are free; happiness and a sense of purpose balance out temptation and despair. Secretly, the golden thread is there; the Lord is present.

In time, we must face and conquer hereditary evils if we are to be reborn. But this is done gradually so that basic happiness can be maintained throughout regeneration. Heavenly delights feed us in every state if we obey the commandments of the Lord. Only one evil is faced at a time, when our character is strong enough to meet it and maintain happiness. Secretly within, the golden thread sustains us with poignant beauty and promise.

Rachel and Leah

Now Laban had two daughters: the name of the elder was Leah, and the name of the younger was Rachel. Leah's eyes were weak, but Rachel was beautiful in form and beautiful in look (Genesis 29:17).

It is through Rachel that Jacob and Laban first meet. She represents the affection of spiritual truth. How could Laban, who depicts our ambitious side, 'father' such a heavenly love? This intermediate self knows the advantage of a knowledge of spiritual truths to gain respect, and it spurs us on to learn them. There has to be this knowledge before the affection for truth can come. Then the Lord provides that, secretly, a genuine affection for spiritual truth is born from our remains. Spiritually, Laban is not the father of Rachel—only apparently so, as in the literal story.

In our normal cycle of moods, in which we experience neither deep joy nor deep sorrow, occasionally may come the most rare and beautiful times of interior delight—states in which we momentarily feel profound happiness. These fleeting moments of inner joy are represented by Rachel, who is "beautiful in form and beautiful in look." Jacob depicts our ordinary cycle of living with its routine and slight joys. The Rachel times give us strength to continue the routine of daily life and enable us to keep fighting evil. No wonder Jacob fell in love with her!

Though Rachel states inspire us, their memory can be frustrating. We cannot help comparing the humdrum routine to the rare moments of profound joy. In our daily life we may be aware of a certain deadness in ourselves; despite efforts to obey our beliefs, we lack inner vitality. The Rachel states can accentuate this deadness and make us realize even more keenly that spiritually we are barely alive.

This is when we may become dedicated to a hope and an ideal. We resolve to find out how to make the rare times of inspiration continual and enduring. This means uniting Rachel and Jacob within us so that our continual efforts to live well are blessed with inner happiness. At this point we realize that the means of attaining everyday spiritual happiness is living according to Divine truth. We also perceive that truths of the inmost realm of the heart and thought are the ones that will gain us our goal. With this comes an affection for interior truth, the pathway to heaven.

This affection for spiritual truth is represented by Jacob's love for Rachel, who was so beautiful. When Jacob and Rachel met "he kissed her, and lifted up his voice and wept."[6] In deepest states of love, we weep for joy. His love for her was immediate and full; we often feel the same way toward interior truth.

When Jacob had been with Laban for a month, helping him with his problems and work, Laban turned to him and said, "because you are my relative, should you therefore serve me for nothing? Tell me, what should your wages be?" Jacob replied: "I will serve you seven years for Rachel your younger daughter."[7]

So Jacob served seven years for Rachel, and they seemed but a few days to him because of the love he had for her. Then Jacob said to Laban, "Give me my woman, for my days are fulfilled, that I may go in to her." And Laban gathered together all the men of the place and made a feast. Now it came to pass in the evening, that he took Leah his daughter and brought her to Jacob; and he went in to her (Genesis 29:21-23).

Jacob has worked loyally for seven years, through a complete cycle of states (seven signifies what is complete). Yet he finds himself deprived of the interior marriage for which he has hoped, for in the darkness of night Laban has brought Leah, not Rachel. Jacob discovers in the morning light that he has been given exterior truths—Leah and not Rachel. He is filled with frustration and asks: "What is this you have done to me? Was it not for Rachel that I served you? Why then have you deceived me?"[8] Laban tells him that in their country the oldest daughter is always married first.

Our struggle for spiritual joy usually takes much longer than we first thought it would. We feel betrayed after working so hard and long. But with reflection on why such joy was withheld, we will see the justice. Our own evils have stopped us short; selfishness blinded us to any interior understanding of the Word. The truths we had learned that seemed so deep were actually very general and sometimes blurred by falsities. Our understanding was nearsighted, like Leah, limited by hereditary evil in the natural. We do not see the most profound truths at first, only those that are most easily grasped. This is in order; it takes time to progress.

Leah represents ideas such as: that we conquer evil through our own spiritual strength unaided by the Lord; that merit for shunning evil is appropriate and right; that ambition for self is good; that pride in family, in status, in our abilities, is justifiable; that we should put self-concern first before others. These ideas are external, but through them we begin the process of rebirth if innocence is present.

After serving another full cycle of states, Jacob was given Rachel. After studying the Word to discover what interior truth actually is, we have to apply this truth to our lives through a fullness of states, through hard times and uplifted times. Then the marriage between Jacob and Rachel takes place; we can be conjoined with the delightful affection of interior truth. Through this marriage, Jacob finds happiness. Finally his everyday life becomes blessed with the vitality of heaven—the inner conjugial, inner uses and inner loves!

Jacob's Flocks

Thus [Jacob] became exceedingly prosperous, and had large flocks, female and male servants, and camels and donkeys (Genesis 30:43).

The natural is progressively reborn. Jacob has son after son—state after state of rebirth. He still works for Laban, even though Laban does not always treat him fairly. The dream of the ladder is being fulfilled with Jehovah's blessings. Our spiritual life grows steadily as we devote ourselves to use and hold to our ideals. We work for many years and gradually reap the fruits of our labors.

Through clever management, Jacob manages to build up a large herd of his own, using Laban's herd to do it. In our work, Laban is the selfish desire for success and position. This ambition for self-glory can be very powerful; it is love of dominion expressing itself. We have no idea at first that this is selfish, seeing it as a desire to serve others. Selfish loves spur us on to learn valuable things. Laban's flocks symbolize the various occupational techniques and skills learned to further our own advancement. Yet as we grow, our developing conscience (Jacob) begins to take these techniques and skills to itself for the sake of true uses, looking to others from mutual love.

Selfish ambition, Laban, can drive us on to learn our occupational tasks thoroughly and perform them expertly. But astonishingly, we may find ourselves beginning to love our work for its own sake. Genuine affections can join themselves with our conscience and our motives for working skillfully can shift.

Gradually this shifting causes an inner conflict. Part of us, Laban, is performing uses entirely for the sake of self-advancement, whereas the Jacob part performs them for the sake of the uses themselves. At first we are not aware of this struggle, not yet believing that there is anything wrong with selfish ambition. Laban is still a friend. But Jacob's possessions become greater and greater. Our unselfish love of uses becomes stronger, and the difference between it and selfish ambition more apparent.

All this time, Rachel has been barren. Finally, "God remembered Rachel, and God listened to her and opened her womb."[9] Joseph is born, the wonder child. This is the beginning of a whole new state, the final major state in regeneration. Joseph symbolizes the love of the Lord truly born and alive in us. In the Writings this is called the celestial of the spiritual. He is the first child of the deeply loved wife. When he is born, changes begin to occur at once.

"Jacob saw the face of Laban, and indeed it was not favorable toward him as before."[10] In the spiritual world, the face portrays exactly the interior loves. At last Jacob sees the true face or interior qualities of Laban. When we have enough strength, the Lord reveals to us the quality of our selfish ambitions. This is a startling revelation. But it should not reduce us to lasting despair, because by this time our conscience is strong enough to stand the shock.

We quickly realize that we must separate ourselves from our selfish ambitions. Jacob flees from Laban, taking his own family and all his possessions. Laban pursues them, but in the end they part amicably. If we do not completely separate from this selfish ambition, we bring grief upon ourselves. The Lord never brings spiritual unhappiness to us, but we can bring it upon ourselves. If we choose to stay with Laban and continue his friendship, regeneration becomes a painful struggle. There has to be a separation of Jacob and Laban for a sense of peace. This separation struggle may continue for a lifetime, or it may come in later maturity for those who deeply "trust in the Lord."

The Land of Israel

Then the Lord said to Jacob, "Return to the land of your fathers and to your nativity, and I will be with you" (Genesis 31:3).

As Jacob nears Canaan, he wrestles with an angel, who changes his name to Israel—meaning the natural self reborn.[11] This brings a sweet peace and conjunction with the angels of the spiritual heaven. In this state, Esau and Jacob become the closest of friends. Esau comes to meet Jacob and they have a beautiful reunion. Esau has priority, for now love rules.[12] We finally attain our wish—spontaneous good inflows into our lives.

While on the journey, Rachel has her second and last child, Benjamin. He is born near Ephrath (Bethlehem). The birth is hard and Rachel dies. But to die, spiritually, is to find new life. Benjamin is a symbol of wonderful new truths, seen from the love Joseph represents. Joseph and Benjamin are together; Benjamin is a medium between Joseph and his brothers, a quality that allows the celestial heaven to inflow fully.[13]

Jehovah speaks to Israel in Bethel:

> I am God Almighty. Be fruitful and multiply; a nation and a company of nations shall proceed from you, and kings shall come from your body. The land which I gave Abraham and Isaac I give to you; and to your descendants after you I give this land (Genesis 35:11-12).

The covenant with Abraham is being fulfilled in Isaac and Jacob-Israel. They have been blessed, through trials and struggles, with love and richness. Israel has come full circle from his ignoble escape from Esau to their tender reunion. He has come back to the land of Canaan, the place of his most innocent loves. The dream of the ladder comes to life.

Like Jacob-Israel, our conscience feels troublesome to us at first, but as it builds in strength it builds in character. It is the means by which we can ascend to the Lord and possess all the qualities we struggled with His aid to attain. Our lives, even on the natural level, can become spiritually and emotionally rich and full. We can have many beloved spiritual children, the results of our years of internal work. They have led us up the ladder to heaven, and now the angels are returning to make earth a paradise. We have left much of our selfishness behind. Finally, we can be blessed with a return to spontaneous good. Esau and Isaac welcome Jacob and his family home.

We sense a beautiful thing: that all this has happened because the Lord stood above the ladder of loves. These spiritual children, and this coming home, are His gifts. He has richly fulfilled the promises of our youthful dreams.

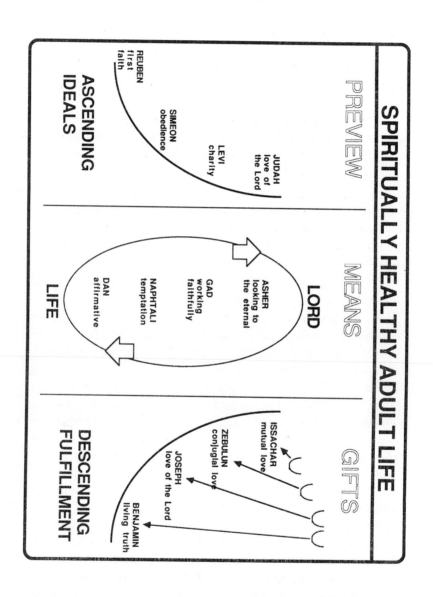

Chapter 14

Ascending and Descending

Then he dreamed, and behold, a ladder was set up on the earth, and its top reached to heaven; and there the angels of God were ascending and descending on it. And behold, the Lord stood above it and said: "I am the Lord God of Abraham your father and the God of Isaac; the land on which you lie I will give to you and your descendants. Also your descendants shall be as the dust of the earth; you shall spread abroad to the sea and to the east, to the north and the south; and in you and in your seed all the families of the earth shall be blessed" (Genesis 28:12-14).

..."And there the angels of God were ascending and descending on it," signifies infinite and eternal communication, and the consequent conjunction; and that from what is lowest there is as it were an ascent, and afterwards when the order is inverted, a descent...(AC 3697).

This dream of Jacob's is an image of spiritual rebirth; everyone can reach the heavenly land the Lord promises to give him. Each one of Jacob-Israel's twelve sons represents a step on the ladder reaching to heaven—the states of our spiritual growth. The number twelve, used so often in the Word, represents heaven as a whole and its twelve constituent parts. It also symbolizes the heaven within each person, and the twelve universal goods and truths that form a church.

As a representative church was to be instituted among the sons of Jacob, it was provided by the Lord that he should have twelve sons, that thus all together might represent all things of the church, and each one his part; and this is why the twelve tribes sprang from them (AE 430:8).

The first ten sons of Jacob were born to Leah and the hand-maids, not to the beloved Rachel. "When Jehovah saw that Leah was unloved, He opened her womb; but Rachel was barren."[1] Our external nature, symbolized by Leah, is difficult to regenerate because "in it are many things which are not in order and are exposed to injuries from the body and the world."[2] Jacob did not want Leah; he wanted to marry the more attractive Rachel right away. However, we are more in tune with external things at first because they can be obviously sensed and are more appropriate to our state. We are joined to the affection for external truth first (Leah) and it enables us to take the initial steps towards rebirth.

The First Steps Upward

Judah is a lion's whelp...
The sceptre shall not depart from Judah,
Nor a lawgiver from between his feet,
Until Shiloh comes;...(Genesis 49:9,10).

"Judah is a lion's whelp." That this signifies innocence with innate forces, is drawn from the signification of a "lion," as being the good of love and the truth thence derived in their power...; thus a "lion's whelp" denotes innocence with forces (AC 6367).

The initial series of sons born to Jacob and Leah are Reuben, Simeon, Levi and Judah. These foretell the overall rebirth of the natural, the general progress which comes before the details follow and infill. They represent a honeymoon state, when applying rational truths to life is still fresh and we are full of vigor. They also symbolize an ascent up the ladder of Jacob's dream.

Reuben, the firstborn, is the initial practical faith in everyday living—the vital first step, "my might and the beginning of my strength, the excellency of dignity and the excellency of power."[3] However, like Reuben, this faith tends to be "unstable as water"[4] unless it is followed by Simeon.

Simeon, named after 'hearing,' is obedience or self-compulsion—putting religion into natural life. This results in a general charity, which is depicted by Levi. Levi is also the affection of truth; his descendants were the priests of the Israelites. He paves the way for Judah.

Judah symbolizes a trusting love of the Lord, which is celestial. This celestial is love of the Lord felt in daily life (the natural). Judah also represents the love of the Most Ancients, pure in childlike innocence. He is the celestial level operating in a general way in the natural. The celestial is active throughout rebirth, here to strengthen the heart for the difficult temptations that follow. Celestial remains reign until Shiloh comes. By Shiloh is meant the Lord being received by the older adult and the tranquility this brings.

> ...By Judah are here represented...they who are in the good of celestial love.... They who are in this love are most closely conjoined with the Lord, and are therefore in the inmost heaven, where they are in a state of innocence, from which they appear to the rest as little children, and wholly as loves in form. Others are not able to go near them, and therefore when they are sent to others, they are encompassed by other angels, by whom the sphere of their love is tempered, which would otherwise throw into a swoon those to whom they are sent; for the sphere of their love penetrates even to the marrows (AC 4750).

What a beautiful picture! Still, this sweet innocence is so strong—the young lion—the highest level of the human heart. Judah depicts the last of the general, preparatory states. These four sons symbolize an ascent to prepare for the rebirth of the natural that now follows.

Means to a Heavenly End

Dan shall judge his people...
Gad, a troop shall tramp upon him,
But he shall triumph at last.
Bread from Asher shall be rich,
And he shall yield royal dainties.
Naphtali is a deer let loose;
He gives goodly words (Genesis 49:16-21).

The next four sons are Dan, Naphtali, Gad and Asher, born to Jacob's handmaids. They represent the means to overcoming selfish ends in natural life and putting on heavenly ends, and thus the means of joining the heavenly and earthly levels of the mind. They are really the key to attaining the heavenly 'self,' which is the proprium given to angels.[5]

But above these four means, and intertwining through them, is the golden thread of remains. Another overall means or presence is the Word, which is the Lord speaking to us, helping us on the way:

> Every man is born into two diabolical loves, the love of self and the love of the world . . . and as man is born into these loves he is also born into evils of every kind . . . . Because man, in respect to his self is such, *means* have been given by the Divine mercy of the Lord by which man can be withdrawn from his [lower] self; these means are given *in the Word*; and when man cooperates with these means, that is, when he thinks and speaks, wills and acts from the Divine Word, he is kept by the Lord in things Divine, and is thus withheld from self; and when this continues there is formed with man by the Lord as it were a new self, both voluntary and intellectual . . . thus man becomes as it were created anew (AE 585a; italics added).

We also have our spiritual freedom:

> Whatever a man does from freedom in accordance with his thought is appropriated to him as his, and remains. This is because *man's proprium and his freedom make one*. Man's proprium belongs to his life; and what a man does from freedom in accordance with reason is appropriated to him as his. It appears to him to be his; nevertheless, the good is not man's own but the Lord's in man (DP 78; italics added).

The Lord gives us remains, the Word and free choice as gifts for our spiritual life. With these, we can progress through the stages represented by Dan, Naphtali, Gad and Asher.

Dan is the *first means*, representing the "affirmative of internal truth."[6] The affirmative principle—affirmative to the Lord, to charity, to internal truth—is essential to spiritual growth. It is a believing, an affirming, the promises of the Lord in the Word. It is the vital step leading to 'all intelligence and wisdom' (cf. AC 2568). Because of this, the tribe Dan had its two dwelling places at entrances to the land of Canaan or heaven. We cannot progress without being willing to look upward. To be affirmative is not naive—it is the expression of all that is good within us from the Lord.

Naphtali is the second son in this series and the *"second general means:"*[7] temptation in which there is victory.[8] All rebirth comes through these triumphs by the Lord in us. Their release and joy is depicted in Jacob's blessing: "Naphtali is a deer let loose: he gives goodly words."[9] After being bound by our troubles like a deer that has been trapped and tied by hunters, Naphtali is the ecstasy of being released and springing into freedom. "Goodly words" of thanks do come spontaneously at such moments.

Spiritual temptations are a necessary part of our rebirth. Yet the Lord governs when and how we go through them so that they do not destroy our basic happiness. During this difficult spiritual work, the Lord is nearer to us than at any other time, guarding us with Divine compassion. Still the reality is that temptations are inwardly painful—deeply painful. Some of the cries of despair in the Psalms express this vividly. To deny this spiritual pain is simply untruthful, and can hinder genuine rebirth.

Before the final victory, we feel despair through which the selfish ego is broken and we become more gentle. 'Ishmael,' the persuasiveness of lower rational thinking, is humbled:

> A state of anxiety and of grief even to despair effects this [softening] .... When they are reduced to such a state that they perceive hell in themselves, and this to such an extent that they despair that they can ever be saved, then for the first time is this persuasive broken, and with it pride, and contempt for others in comparison with themselves...(AC 2694:2,4).

We have to feel humility before we can find the Lord. But that does not mean sinking completely down and denying all joy. There is a basic deep peace within, and after the trial comes the release of spiritual victory. "Naphtali is a deer let loose."

Gad, the third general means,[10] is *works:*[11]

> The Lord's kingdom commences in man from the life which is of works, for he is then in the beginning of regeneration; but when the Lord's kingdom is in a man, it terminates in works, and then the man is regenerate.... Jesus loved John more than the rest; for by John were represented good works (AC 3934:7).

Works include one's occupation and all other expressions of one's inner use or endowment. As the Jacob-Laban relationship shows, we are reborn through true works. Within such works our inner use or love comes into outer actions. Use so expressed brings the Lord to us, and perhaps above all else is the proper means of rebirth because of its great power:

> In the degree that a man is in the love of use, he is in the Lord, in that degree also he loves Him and loves the neighbor, and in that degree is he a man.... The reason loving the Lord means to do uses from Him and for His sake is that all the good uses a man does are from the Lord; good uses are "goods," and the latter, it is well-known, are from the Lord; and loving them is to do them, for what a man loves, that he does. There is no other way in which the Lord can be loved, for *uses, which are goods, are from the Lord and are therefore Divine*, or rather, they are the Lord Himself with man (DLDW 35,36; italics added).

The inmost of uses is found in conjugial love: the "superior excellence of its use is above all other uses."[12] So conjugial love would be the highest of all means to attain the heavenly proprium. If we look to the Lord, falling in love is only an introduction to states of gradually increasing happiness and use.[13] The highest image of the heavenly self or proprium is the regenerate married couple, and the truest 'self' is the 'one angel' who is husband and wife. They know that this 'self' is God's gift to them.

The *fourth means* to the true or heavenly proprium is depicted by *Asher*:[14] "being content in God."[15] As we grow, our idea of blessedness or being content changes. Babies feel blessed by their mother's milk, children by toys. The blessings we delight in become more internal as we progress spiritually. The crown of these is to feel a trusting love of the Lord.

When we first choose 'life'—the pathway to rebirth—the beautiful jewel of eternal happiness is placed within the home of our spirit. Because of our external nature and bodies and the mental barriers they cause, we are only vaguely aware of the fire and light of this jewel. We cannot feel the ecstasy of angelic happiness, but enough warmth and light penetrate to us at times to give us a serene 'content in God.'

> ... While in the body, man is in worldly cares and consequent anxieties that prevent the happiness of eternal life (which is deep within him) from then being manifested in any other way [than as] a kind of obscure delight (AC 3938:7).

Given or having discovered basic mental health, we can keep our 'cares and anxieties' to a minimum by rightly prioritizing our lives. Anne Morrow Lindbergh explores this beautifully in *Gift from the Sea*.[16] The pace of modern life is busy, yet often has its own real delights. But we should get off the merry-go-round of 'busyness' once in a while! If we keep our priorities focused on what is eternal, we will not be overly burdened by anxious, 'conscience monger' spirits, or by other sensuous spirits who take away internal peace.[17]

We will begin to feel spontaneous delight in small, external things such as working in the garden or walking in a woods. Gradually this expands into an inner delight at our spiritual foundations. Then comes Asher's meditative sense of contentment with our lot. This is the ultimate of heaven within us.

> From his hill-slopes, the man of Asher could cast his longing eyes over the enchanting blue expanse of the Mediterranean—in semblance of one's wistful yearning for that eternal world which one can hardly visualize from within the barriers of space and time (*The Divine Allegory*, p. 110).[18]

Dan is the beginning means—being affirmative to internal truths, and Asher is the culminating means, in which the joy of the heavenly proprium is beginning to be *felt*. The heart is coming alive. The Dan quality is affirmative to the teaching that a current pulls us toward the Lord; Asher feels its joy! In fact, the Lord's message to the New Church is one of buoyancy and joy. Asher represents receiving blessedness in the externals of our hearts and thoughts.[19]

The universal means to the heavenly proprium and its release into spiritual joy is the willingness to compel ourselves to obey Divine truth. This is represented by Jacob. The father of these other means, self-compulsion (Jacob), has freedom within it and expresses above all else a genuine humility.[20] Through faithful obedience, Jacob becomes Israel and each of his sons is a blessing.

The Final Steps

Zebulun shall dwell by the haven of the sea;
He shall become a haven for ships...
Issachar is a strong donkey,
Lying down between two burdens;
He saw that rest was good,
And that the land was pleasant...
Joseph is the son of a fruitful one,
The son of a fruitful one over a fountain...
    (Gen. 49:13-15,22).

The final four sons of Jacob are states of regeneration: Issachar, Zebulun, Joseph, and Benjamin. They are the culmination of our spiritual life. In a joyful opening up and infilling, the Lord leads us upwards into spiritual heights. We simultaneously descend to orderly ultimates that are filled with delights. Even the lowest level of the senses is brought into alignment with the highest level of the mind, and the sensuous flowers into new life. These final four sons promise what 'may be'—either on earth for the very faithful, or else in heaven. The Lord's desire, however, is to have those states come "as in heaven so upon the earth."

Issachar contains the first hint of this rebirth. Initially, he depicts a state of 'hire'—working only for natural rewards such as money, position and respect. But his other meaning, with rebirth, is mutual love. This love for others makes religion real and is the inspiration for use. At last there is real, enduring love for others—a sweetness in friendship and companionship.

With Zebulun, we feel a kind of conjugial love never experienced before—the fulfillment of betrothal's dreams—a lasting inner union. Conjugial love is a gift from the Lord, given only through temptation and victory, in which our spirit perceives that all that is good and true is from God. It is a regenerating and regenerate love, felt early in receptive states given by the Lord and coming later in the regeneration of the natural—the Zebulun state.

This is shown in the place and correspondence of the tribe of Zebulun in the land of Canaan. In glorifying the natural, Jesus made it possible for conjugial love to be received on the natural plane in us. He brought warmth and light, the conjugial marriage of good and truth, to this plane. When He began His ministry, He left Nazareth and:

> ...He came and dwelt in Capernaum, which is by the sea, in the regions of Zebulun and Naphtali, that it might be fulfilled which was spoken by Isaiah the prophet saying:
> "The land of Zebulun and the land of Naphtali,
> The way of the sea, beyond the Jordan,
> Galilee of the Gentiles:
> The people who sat in darkness saw a great light,
> And upon those who sat in the region and shadow of death
> Light has dawned" (Matthew 4:13-16).

Finally, after the ten sons have been born, Rachel conceives her first child. She was barren because internal truths cannot be perceived until regeneration is well advanced. Now the stage has been set for the affection of internal truth to give birth to inmost love of the Lord. After Zebulun, who represents conjugial love newly felt in our natural life, comes a beautiful integration—a conjunction of the inner and outer heart.

> This conjunction cannot come forth until the natural or external man has been prepared, that is, until it has received and acknowledged the general truths signified by the ten sons of Jacob by Leah and the handmaids; and until the good of the natural man has been conjoined with the truths

therein.....After this conjunction has been effected, the interior man and the exterior enter into the heavenly marriage...(AC 3969).

Then Joseph is born. He symbolizes a wise love of the Lord, called the celestial of the spiritual. From this love our heavenly self or heavenly proprium can grow. When he rises to full power within us, we become completely reborn. Every level within us is free, fully creative and in balance with the other planes. Our outer life becomes a total, beautiful expression of what is in our heart. Hereditary and former actual evils have been removed by the Lord with man's cooperation, and these evils are now on the periphery of the mind. They are held by the Lord in a basic quiescence.

All that is needed is "little Benjamin, their leader,"[21] the "beloved of the Lord."[22] He and Joseph belong together because they symbolize deeply felt love of the Lord, and sparkling truths seen from this love.[23] They are the only two sons of Rachel, the affection of spiritual truth. They are the internal things of the church, while their brothers are the external.[24] Benjamin is:

...the spiritual truth which is from celestial good, which [good, is represented by] "Joseph." Both, therefore, taken together, are that intermediate which is between the spiritual man and the celestial man. But this good and this truth are distinct from the celestial which is represented by "Judah," and from the spiritual which is represented by "Israel"; the former is higher or more interior, and the latter is lower or more exterior...(AC 4592:2).

Benjamin is the medium; without him Joseph cannot reveal himself to his other brothers. Benjamin's sparkling new truths give us the ability to make the final transition. With him, the whole mind comes to love the 'Joseph' within and allows him to rule.

The Dream Fulfilled

"Behold, I am with you and will keep you wherever you go, and will bring you back to this land; for I will not leave you until I have done what I have spoken to you" (Genesis 28:15).

Jacob's dream of the ladder, with the angels ascending and descending before the throne of God, is fulfilled totally in Joseph and Benjamin. His other sons are the steps and states that lead up to that final goal, and the means to it. Together, all twelve of them present the fullness of all the universal goods and truths: heaven in its beauty.

> How good are thy tents, O Jacob,
> Thy tabernacles, O Israel!
> As the valleys are they planted,
> As gardens by the river;
> As the sandal trees which the Lord hath planted,
> As cedar trees beside the waters (*Liturgy*, p. 579).[25]

When we are born, the highest celestial angels descend and take care of us while we are in the obscure sensual state of infancy. As we ascend into the spiritual level of childhood, the spiritual angels descend to us. Adolescence eventually brings the step into rationality and the company of natural angels. In the process of rebirth in adult life, outwardly we descend the ladder and yet simultaneously ascend in our hearts. First the rational is reformed. That is, we come to see that Divine truth is true! And we feel a sparkling delight in this discovery. This is represented by Isaac replacing Ishmael. The delights we feel then are from the lowest angels. When we allow the Lord to reform the natural level—the life of Jacob—we again come into the company of spiritual angels. They gift us with a new love of others. Finally, as even the lowest sensual plane is cleansed and reordered, the highest angels return to us, and gift us with a wonderful love of the Lord Himself.

Each plane of the ladder waits for the ascent and descent of rebirth to become complete. With regeneration, the ladder is a one, with the Lord standing above—the source of all life, love and warmth. No one step of the ladder is focused on as the key degree: not the natural or daily-life level, nor the rational or spiritual-doctrinal level. The ladder rises in unity to God, with angels ascending and descending in the beautiful flow of influx and reception in uses. For example, in conjugial love (Zebulun), delights are felt on every step of the ladder, and uses of each level refine the whole. Finally there comes a picture of life so complete and beautiful that we can only fall down and worship our Lord.

By getting caught intellectually or emotionally on any one level of the ladder, we can fail to see the balanced perspective of the whole. If we are only concerned with the natural, emotional or 'gut' level, we cannot see or feel the joyous heights of spiritual love. Yet, we may achieve the Isaac rational and fail to descend again into charity in life. Then we only see spiritual truths but fail to apply them to make them alive. Every level has its power and importance; each is vital to the whole.

To really come alive on all levels, our first step is the affirmative attitude of Dan, including affirmation of Divine doctrine. If there is ever a looking upward at revealed spiritual truths in a negative way from the natural emotional level, this is eating of the tree of the knowledge of good and evil. This is to go only by what we sense and feel: "to say in the heart that we cannot believe them (spiritual things) until we are convinced by what we can apprehend, or perceive by the senses."[26] If we stay only at our natural feelings, we ignore our higher heart and mind.

To be truly human, we must be reborn on every plane. Then, the Lord accomplishes a miracle—he creates a *wise* child. This Joseph state is better than states in infancy, because it comes with full awareness. Once the successive order is within, then the most potent affections shine in the natural and sensuous levels, like diamonds in their settings. The reborn sensuous contains all the other levels within it; here is the power of ultimates. We sense and feel the Lord in nature, and in our ordered sensations. Heaven comes and touches the outmost sensations of life.

Above creation is the Lord, whose Divinely Human love brings all levels to life. Innocence leads to the heavenly self or proprium; to be truly human, we must be willing to turn to Him and be led by Him. In leading us to rebirth, the Lord is first conceived, and then born, within our hearts. Then we feel a nearness to Him not known before. He comes first to the celestial and spiritual in our minds—in Judah and Jerusalem, and then to the natural—to the seashore and mountaintop of Galilee—completely and intimately present. Our Divine

Father is with us in His rational, His natural, and even His glorified body.[27] This glorified body, the Lord present in our natural and sense-life, caused Thomas to exclaim in wonder: "my Lord and my God" (John 20: 28).

Chapter 15

"This Dreamer Is Coming"

A son of a fruitful one is Joseph,
A son of a fruitful one by a fountain;
By the hands of the Mighty God of Jacob...
By the God of your father who will help you,
And by the Almighty who will bless you
With blessings of heaven above,
Blessings of the deep that lies beneath,
Blessings of the breasts and of the womb.
The blessings of your father
Have excelled the blessings of my ancestors,
Up to the utmost bound of the everlasting hills.
They shall be on the head of Joseph,
And on the crown of the head of him who was separate from
 his brothers (Genesis 49:22-26).

Joseph is the dreamer in the sense of true, eternal dreams. He leads the way to the arms and heart of the Lord, the discovering of the warmth of life that we have inwardly prayed for. In the supreme sense, he symbolizes the celestial of the spiritual in the Lord—an inmost love for others.[1] It follows that in the spiritual sense, which deals with our regeneration, Joseph is our highest love for another and so our love of the Lord. He is the reawakening of the remains of innocence from infancy now conjoined to a new quality—innocent celestial love in older age. This is the highest regenerate good.

The heart of remains from infancy is the love of the Lord. Around this 'tree of life' is planted a garden of gentle and unselfish loves. Why are these remains so poignant—why do they haunt us like the memory of Eden? Simply because this was a time in our lives when our will was mostly good. Hereditary evil was kept subordinate, sometimes even quiescent, by the Lord. Unworried and uncalculating, we had heavenly love and delight in our heart. The world was alive with the wonder of love and the miracles of nature.

To the Most Ancient Church, the natural world was a land of heavenly wonder. This celestial race knew the science of correspondences from innate perception; without any instruction they perceived the spiritual correspondence of everything they saw. To them, nature was a garden of Eden—another heaven. They loved to look at the brooks and fields, at the trees and mountains and sky; for though they looked upon this world, they saw heaven. Through perception of nature's symbols, their spirits were raised into heaven so that they were able to be with angels.

Because of their perception of correspondences, the Most Ancients needed no written revelation; they learned through communication with angels. Nature itself was also their Word; everything in it spoke to them of heavenly truth and good. At the time of the flood, however, most of the celestial genius perished from the earth. A whole world fell, a world of inner vision. Nature lost its wondrous use as the living Word.

This does not mean that we can never again see the Lord and heavenly things in nature. We no longer approach nature with an inborn knowledge of correspondences; but we *can* approach, to study and wonder, with enlightened reason and inner love. We can learn correspondences and apply them lovingly. If we perceive nature this way, then it will again become a Divine theater, a beautiful representation of heaven and God.

When we reach adulthood, there are still good loves with us. These are implanted in the understanding, not in the hereditary will. Almost all of our adult life is lived in the sphere of our understanding. It seems that we cannot go back to living from the will, for apparently the garden of Eden implanted in childhood has been lost. Instead of innocence in our will, we find treachery—the selfishness that was held at bay in childhood. However, remains are in our understanding; they form the basis of the new will which will be in the understanding.

With Joseph a new heavenly love is born within us that comes when the Israel state of mind is in its old age. This love brings a new sight of the Lord, not just in the spiritual plane of the mind, but dawning upon our very senses, which are touched by the celestial. The Lord is seen within nature and even within natural sciences with a new power and beauty. Nature becomes alive, touched by a wonder and inner beauty not perceived before. Implicitly it is known: this creation "is the Lord's doing; it is marvelous in our eyes" (Psalm 118:23).

This vision is represented by the coat of many colors that Israel gave to Joseph to express his fatherly love. Each color is symbolic of some part of nature or science. Put together, they clothe the Lord, appearing in nature's kingdoms. In an applied sense, each color symbolizes a natural science, such as physics, anatomy, biology, astronomy and medicine. As we regenerate, we can come into a penetrating vision. We see every science, every part of nature, as an ultimate clothing of the Lord Himself, a beautiful coat of many colors.

We can all see the Lord within nature to some degree: at times in childhood, and as adults, when remains of good are strongly active; these are states of the golden thread. Then by looking with an open heart and eyes at a tree, a flower, the ocean, the stars, the perception of our Creator inflows. This is not merely intellectual, it is a deep love for mountains and mountain streams, for oceans or lakes sparkling in sunlight, for the beauty and fragrance of spring days. We seldom consciously associate such delights with the Lord. Nevertheless, the joy given is from Him and is based on inner, secret influx.

Joseph's childhood, as the beloved son of Jacob, was full of this innocence and delight. He dreamt that the sheaves of the field bowed before him, and then the sun, moon and eleven stars. These symbolized his family's bowing. But these dreams do not seem to come true as his brothers turn against him.

When his brothers saw that Israel loved Joseph more than themselves they were inflamed with jealousy. Joseph followed after them to Dothan, and they took away his coat and cast him into a deep pit that was "empty, there was no water in it."[2] This is the pit of denial, where there is no truth—no water. Here the brothers represent self-love and conceit. These qualities use science and nature not to confirm the Lord's existence, but to disprove it. They sold Joseph to traders bound for Egypt. Then they took his coat, dipped it in blood, and brought it to their father, saying:

> "We have found this. Do you know whether it is your son's tunic or not?" And he recognized it and said, "It is my son's tunic. A wild beast has devoured him. Without a doubt Joseph is torn to pieces." .... And all his sons and all his daughters arose to comfort him; but he refused to be comforted, and he said, "For I shall go down into the grave to my son in mourning." Thus his father wept for him (Genesis 37:32-35).

It seems that early childhood remains are destroyed by hereditary evil. The veil of innocence is removed when we enter adulthood. Tendencies to selfishness flood upon us that we never dreamt possible in a more innocent childhood. With the entrance into adult life, childhood remains are caught up to an inner protective sphere above natural consciousness. When evil is active, it appears that they are dead. Israel believes that Joseph is torn to pieces.

> That "Joseph is torn in pieces" signifies . . . that the internal celestial has perished by evils and falsities. That "to be torn in pieces" has this signification, is because in the spiritual world there is no other tearing in pieces than that of good by evils and falsities. The case herein is like death and what relates to death. In the spiritual sense these do not signify natural death, but spiritual death, which is damnation, for there is no other death in the spiritual world.... Moreover, the wild beasts which tear, signify . . . evils . . . and falsities, which also are represented by wild beasts in the other life (AC 5828:1).

No matter what the appearance, we are still influenced by early remains even when they are withdrawn. Their influx enables us to think rationally and to choose good. We no longer feel the remains in their earliest power, but they allow us in freedom to compel our lower nature into submission. We do not 'tear' apart remains and their perceptions unless we choose to:

It is a universal law that influx adjusts itself according to efflux [i.e., according to what we do], and if efflux is checked, influx is checked. Through the internal man there is an influx of good and truth from the Lord, and through the external there must be an efflux, namely into the life, that is, in the exercise of charity. Where there is this efflux, then there is continual influx from heaven.... Whereas if there is resistance in the external man, it follows... that the internal through which is the influx is closed. Through this closing there comes stupidity in spiritual things, even until the man... at last becomes insane, so that he opposes falsities against truths,... and evils against goods.... Thus he tears good completely to pieces (AC 5828:3).

Benjamin

Of Benjamin he said:
"The beloved of the Lord shall dwell in safety by Him,
Who shelters him all the day long;
And he shall dwell between His shoulders"
(Deuteronomy 33:12).

Jacob learns to live with the apparent death of Joseph, to continue his life with some equanimity. In the beginning of regeneration of the natural level, self-compulsion in shunning evil shows loyalty to our remains, and holds open a quiet influx from them. Remains are not known as they were in childhood, but at least the distant memory of them can be preserved, and the hope that some day they can be rediscovered in fullness. In these states, hereditary evil is with us, but it does not dominate. We are in the valley of shadow, but the Lord is with us. The Word and its sphere give us a warmth and light, and hope is preserved for a return to the mountain peaks of childhood.

As the years go by, earliest remains are not rediscovered, even though we remain faithful. We find a lesser good, the 'good of truth,' that still gives us something of heaven that is rich and rewarding. Spontaneous delight in truth replaces former self-compulsion. There is a love of the neighbor, a compassion, that warms the heart. This is a new love placed within the heart, not the celestial good of remains, but real love of others given after years of self-discipline. It brings heaven—the spiritual angels to our heart.

From this spiritual good implanted in us spring living perceptions of truth—Benjamin. He becomes the new favorite son of Jacob:

> The man who is being regenerated . . . is first led to good by means of truth; for man does not know what spiritual good . . . is, except through truth or through doctrine drawn from the Word. In this way he is initiated into good. Afterward, when he has been initiated, he no longer is led *to good through truth*, but *to truth through good*; for he then not only sees from good the truths which he knew before, but also from good brings forth new truths, which he did not and could not know before. For good is attended with a longing for truths, because with these it is, as it were, nourished, it being perfected by them. These new truths *differ greatly* from the truths which he had previously known. For those which he then knew had but little life, while those which he has now acquired have life from good (AC 5804:1; italics added).

Once this spiritual good is attained, we come in our hearts to the hilltops of heaven, seeing vistas of truth as new and living. This is the joy of Benjamin. With this vision of 'new truth,' we actually enter the spiritual heaven as to our spirits. We have found the holy grail and left the valleys of earthly life. How beautiful this new world is no one can objectively define; it is within, a thing of the heart and life. Its joy is found in the words of the man formerly blind: " . . . one thing I know, that though I was blind, now I see."[3]

Above the spiritual level of heaven, in the height of heights, is the celestial—that heaven that is the special care of the Lord, where the warmth of spring and summer is continually in the heart, where we find early childhood peace and trust that we thought dead. Spiritual good, and new truth from it, are beautiful on the plane of the understanding. Celestial good is of the will, our very inmost. Those in the celestial heaven live from the will, from love itself, and not from the intellect. The celestial is foretasted when it is loaned to us in infancy. But the Lord wishes us to know and feel this again. He wishes us to recapture innocence and trust, and find a complete love of Him, for this is the highest of spiritual health.

163

The highest level for rebirth in the new age is the celestial of the spiritual. This level is represented by Joseph, who seems to be dead. Here is the new reborn will, that replaces the old one. This new will is in the separated understanding, yes, but now that understanding is transformed. The realm of spiritual good is the outer chamber, where we must abide and prepare before we can go forward. Within our hearts we must face the last temptations, the last spiritual battles, before Joseph is fully revealed to us.

In Egypt

> We have a father, an old man, and a child of his old age, who is young; and his brother is dead (Genesis 44:20).

Years went by without word of Joseph, so that gradually even his brothers came to believe that he had died while in Egypt. Egypt, or certain people there, represents the sensual in this case, which is the last level to be reborn. The resistance to the celestial there is terrible—frighteningly strong. The unregenerate sensuous hates the Lord and hates the celestial. The celestial of remains is not dead, but it goes through great struggles in the plane of the senses.

Joseph is a slave in Potiphar's house. He refuses to commit adultery with his master's wife and she has him thrown into prison. There he meets a butler and a baker, and he interprets their dreams. These two have to do with:

> . . . a state of temptations, by which even bodily things might be brought into correspondence. Bodily things . . . are sensuous things, which are of two kinds, some being subordinate to the intellectual, and some to the will. Those which are subordinate to the intellectual are represented by the butler of the king of Egypt, and those which are subordinate to the will are represented by the baker. That the former are . . . retained, but the latter cast out, is represented by the butler returning to his place and the baker being hanged (AC 5072).

Sight is subject to the intellect, hearing to both will and intellect but mainly intellect, smell and taste to both, and touch to the will.[4] We have two wills: the one we inherit, and the one implanted with remains and nourished by good. The new will is built up in our intellect or understanding. The baker represents the bodily delights stirred through touch, taste and smell. Evil is especially appealing when the senses are allied with the old will. The new will affects these also, but finds a powerful enemy trying to interfere—hereditary evil.

We may think of spiritual temptations as being on an inner plane. However, they are also on the physical or sensuous plane; both levels need to be purified. Interior evils often find sensuous clothing. The Writings make clear that the final battle of regeneration, the great Armageddon, is on the sensuous plane. Interior cleansing is vital, but unless the exterior is also cleansed, heaven cannot descend to ultimates. The inmost of heaven within us is kept bound in the interiors, like Joseph was captive in prison.

In the beginning of rebirth, temptations through the senses are not subtle. The most powerful delights of touch are those that belong to conjugial love, or its opposite. We recognize the perversion of this sense most easily, but have the hardest time defeating it. Adultery, obscenity and lasciviousness are the age-old enemies of the regenerating spirit. The attraction of lust is very strong because it is the perversion of a celestial love, and because it operates through the sense of touch that is especially open to domination by the fallen will. Also, a celestial perversion always masks itself in apparent innocence—what is apparently sweeter than adultery, or more deadly?

The delights of smell and taste center on food and drink. Gluttony, alcoholism and drug abuse pull at our spirit. Food, alcohol and drugs have their uses. We may think that overindulgence is not so bad because it is something we do to our bodies; inside we are fine. However, these abuses are the ultimates for interior evils and subtle defeats that we may not recognize. These are defeats of our love and trust in the Lord and His Word. If we stop outer manifestations of evil, the inner despair lifts as well.[5] Disciplining the senses, so that they serve instead of master us, invites Joseph into our hearts. We *can* come to love others more than ourselves.

In the last stages of rebirth, the temptations on the sensuous plane are very subtle. They center on the illusion of the body that it lives of itself, independent of the Lord. The instinct for self-preservation has its root here. It was the final illusion Jesus overcame on the cross. These last struggles are with inmost pride, with a subtle but powerful sense of merit. They are not struggles as we usually know them, but on a more interior, all-pervasive plane. They concern the new truth symbolized by Benjamin. Part of us is unwilling to ascribe this living truth to the Lord and instead wants to own it. The last battle with pride is all-searching, profound, and can be frightening. In Jesus' life, it was the crucifixion. In His final victories, His bodily senses were ordered, and then glorified. We can also go through this last temptation and purification, although few attain these heights. Yet it is this to which we are called.

Joseph is not released from prison until the sensuous plane is cleansed. The Divine is in the five senses; they are formed by Him. When they are in order they have the highest uses. In each sensuous delight that is in order there is a ladder of delights—moral, rational, spiritual and celestial—leading to the Lord Himself. All degrees are connected by direct correspondence, and they rest and are in their fullness in the sensuous ultimate. When the sensuous is in order, Joseph is released to interpret Pharaoh's dream and rise to power.

Joseph is not only made ruler under Pharaoh, but his plan to preserve Egypt is put into effect. Food is stored up in the seven years of plenty, and, when famine comes, when the sensual puts up its last strong rebellion, all the world comes to Joseph. His ten brothers come and kneel before him, partly fulfilling his first dreams. He conceals his identity from them at first and asks about their father and Benjamin. Judah, or what is genuine in us, tells him that Joseph is dead.

Joseph commands that they return and bring back Benjamin. Without him, Joseph cannot be revealed to his brothers:

> The truth from the Divine, which is "Joseph," cannot have communication with the truths . . . of the natural, which are the "sons of Jacob," without the medium represented by "Benjamin . . . ." As the sons of Jacob were without Benjamin, that is, without the medium, Joseph could not manifest himself to his brothers . . . (AC 5411).

Resurrection

And Joseph could not restrain himself before all those who stood by him.... And he wept aloud.... Then Joseph said to his brothers, "I am Joseph..." (Genesis 45:1,2,3).

Once Benjamin is with the brothers, Joseph can reveal himself to them. Benjamin takes on a deeper meaning when he is with Joseph:

"Benjamin" represents new truth.... This truth is the truth which is from spiritual good, which is "Israel," and which "Benjamin" represents when with his father, but he represents a still more interior truth when he is with Joseph (AC 5806).

Once the brothers recover from shock and see that Joseph is not only alive but has forgiven them, they have a tender reunion. Joseph sends for Jacob, and Pharaoh welcomes the whole family (all seventy of them) into Egypt. This gathering to Joseph is the fruition of regeneration. The celestial is implanted completely on each plane. A wonderful love of others is implanted in the entire mind. We become fully, deeply alive.

We see that the Joseph within us has not died, but become a ruler in 'Egypt.' Our celestial remains and love of the Lord have survived in spite of struggles. Finally, this love—this reality—will rule over science (Egypt). We will come to see, with open hearts, that nature *is* a clothing of Divine wisdom. As nature was once alive and filled with the wonder of heaven, so it will be again. This time, the inner wonder will be unfolded before our enlightened rational and our newborn senses together.

The Golden Thread

And he carried me away in the Spirit to a great and high mountain, and showed me the great city, the holy Jerusalem, descending out of heaven from God, having the glory of God. And her light was like a most precious stone, like a jasper stone, clear as crystal.... And the construction of its wall was of jasper; and the city was pure gold, like clear glass (Revelation 21:10,11,18).

The Lord, in His glorified Divine Human, touches us in each state of our lives, especially in infancy. Remains are implanted that are to lead the way to heaven; the golden thread is started. As we grow, the Lord again and again draws near and touches us, continuing that golden thread, restirring the celestial within each descending plane.

In adult life, free choice is laid before us. Remains counterbalance hereditary evil and we are left in spiritual freedom. If we look to the Lord by shunning evil and praying to Him, remains again inflow. First come the remains from youth, giving the perception that truth is true. Then the remains of childhood enable the natural to be reborn. Finally, the remains of infancy bring celestial life to the sensual. On each plane, knowledges from the Word are implanted in the secret heavenly loves present from youth, childhood and infancy; the golden thread continues.[6]

When Joseph makes himself known to his brothers, he cannot help weeping. It is the weeping of love so deeply moved that tears must come. This is one of the most poignant scenes in the Word; it represents the culmination of regeneration, the goal of life from infancy. The Lord would lead us from the innocence of infancy to the innocence of wisdom: by means of the one, He would lead to the other. The golden thread leads to Joseph, celestial love, being known and loved by his eleven brothers.[7]

We come into a heavenly life we never realized possible. Former feelings of identity, of self, are either left behind or are wonderfully integrated. The false self of hereditary evil is gone, subordinated and held forever subservient by the Lord. Mediate good states that have served as means are also left behind. The innocence of infancy, and all other remains of childhood, are integrated into a one, a unity. Finally, we become again a little child, but a wise child—wise from the Lord alone.

> At that time the disciples came to Jesus, saying, "Who then is greatest in the kingdom of heaven?" And Jesus called a little child to Him, set him in the midst of them, and said, "Assuredly, I say to you, unless you are converted and become as little children, you will by no means enter the kingdom of heaven. Therefore whoever humbles himself as this little child is the greatest in the kingdom of heaven" (Matthew 18:1-4).

Chapter 16

Growing Young

... Jesus called them to Him and said, "Let the little children come to Me, and do not forbid them; for of such is the kingdom of God. Assuredly, I say to you, whoever does not receive the kingdom of God as a little child will by no means enter it" (Luke 18:16-17).

Man is so created as to be during his childhood in external innocence, and when he becomes old in internal innocence, to the end that he may come by means of the former into the latter, and from the latter return to the former. For the same reason when a man becomes old he dwindles in body and becomes like a child, but like a wise child, that is, an angel, for a wise child is in an eminent sense an angel (HH 278:3).

"In a word, to grow old in heaven is to grow young."[1] Aging on earth can be looked at in two ways: from time, or above it; from the standpoint of years, or of states. All of our growth towards regeneration on earth is toward becoming young in spirit. Old age can be by far the happiest time of life. This will be the case in the future New Church on earth. Although outwardly aging, we can internally drink of the fountain of youth. For to be reborn is to enter heaven in heart even while on earth, and to enter its youth:

Those that are in heaven are continually advancing towards the spring of life, with a greater advance towards a more joyful and happy spring the more thousands of years they live; and this to eternity, with increase according to the growth and degree of their love, charity and faith. Women who have died old and worn out with age, if they have lived in faith in the Lord, in charity to the neighbor, and in happy marriage love with a husband, advance with the succession of years more and more into the flower of youth and early womanhood and into a beauty that transcends every conception of any such beauty as is seen on earth. Goodness and charity are what give this form and thus manifest their own likeness, causing the joy and beauty of charity to shine forth from every least particular of the face, and causing them to be very forms of charity (HH 414).

Old age is ideally 'wise infancy,' innocent and playful. Just because this is very rare today does not mean that it cannot exist, or will not gradually increase as the new age progresses. The pathetic condition of some old people today, their deterioration of mind and body, is a testimonial to the sad spiritual state of mankind. We need the healing truths that make us young in spirit, and also progress in the field of geriatrics that will support this goal.

Why do our natural bodies have to age and cause so much suffering? Seeing senile or disabled loved ones may make us wonder what could possibly be the use of this physical disintegration. Why does the Lord allow this helpless and apparently hopeless state?

"Old age" in the internal sense does not signify old age, because the internal man, or man's spirit, does not know what old age is; but as the body or external man grows old, the internal passes into newness of life, man's spirit being perfected by age as his bodily powers diminish (AC 4676).

Remains are implanted all through our lives. In fact, rebirth brings us back into the company of the highest angels who again fill us with their innocent, child-like affections. Although a permission and not ideal order, senility is also a form of being a child. Even though there may not be any evident wisdom in senility, there is innocence. The Lord may permit this to instill a certain kind of remains. Senility often brings a return to outward infancy and helplessness. This is also a return to association with sensuous states, and the celestial angels who operate into such infantile sensuous states. So the Lord can be doing work in secret, preparing those who are senile for greater use in heaven.

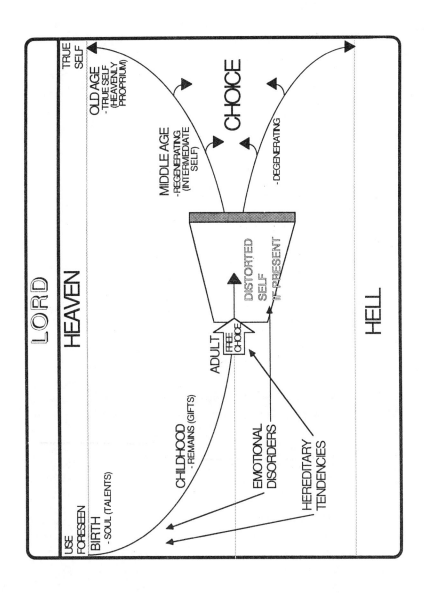

Growing old gracefully is part of the art of living a trusting spiritual life. The body's gradual decay is a natural prod to spiritual growth—there must be something better than this! The pain and disabilities of aging make it easier to accept the idea of the body's death, almost forcing us to think about what lies beyond the shell of our natural lives. Aging of the body helps to propel us toward wisdom of the spirit, if we open our hearts in trust in the Lord. Despair, grouchiness, in fact evil itself, attack strongly in old age. But if faced and overcome from the Lord, the gift that follows gives all of life a tender, eternal meaning.

"Wings Like Eagles"

He gives power to the weak,
And to those who have no might He increases strength.
Even the youths shall faint and be weary,
And the young men shall utterly fall,
But those who wait on the Lord
Shall renew their strength;
They shall mount up with wings like eagles,
They shall run and not be weary, They shall walk and not
   faint (Isaiah 40:30-31).

In every stage of life, there are attitudes that make us 'old' spiritually, there are confirmations of the hereditary love of self. Disobedience goes against the 'Isaac' state of spiritual perception. Hatred is 'anti-Israel,' killing the desire to apply truth to life and so loving others. Nursing hatred and enjoying it in malicious gossip make us hard. The love of dominating over others destroys the 'Joseph' love of the Lord. To dream only of glory and reputation for self narrows our vision and ages us spiritually. It is not necessarily the physically old who have rigid, old spirits.

The wounds of emotional and mental disorders can cause temporary spiritual oldness. Power-worship, narcissism or a false conscience's idol of perfectionism narrow the mind. Undiscovered guilt blocks the ability to grow 'young.' According to bioenergetic theory, these emotional blocks have physical symptoms as well, usually rigidity in certain muscles. Even our body becomes stiffer and 'older' with emotional disorders.

We can also get caught in the trap of mediate good, staying on with 'Laban' long after it is time to separate. The intermediate self then confirms and nurses merit, demanding rewards. This 'me first' attitude is void of real life and saps the vitality of truly reaching out to others and the Lord.

Rigid attitudes calcify our inner selves and create an old spirit. But those who are inwardly young are open to interior truths. And the effect of living these truths gives them the strength spiritually to "mount up with wings like eagles, they shall run and not be weary, they shall walk and not faint."[2]

> There are spirits who are in other respects good, but who cannot as yet be admitted into heaven, because they are not willing to hear and to admit the interior and [still less] the more interior things of the Word.... As upon earth there will, as I think, be many who will hate the interior and more inward things of the Word, because they more closely touch the life of their love ... besides this, they are not willing to be disquieted by such things as [they assert] they are not capable of understanding.... Those spirits were represented to me by a vision—they were like an old woman with an ugly face, but of a snowy white; the face was irregular [in its features], and anything but beautiful; in a word, it was deformed although of a shining white ... whereas, those spirits who hear, admit, and love interior things, were afterwards represented to me by a virgin in a white shining garment, in the very prime of her maiden age, playing on a musical instrument. Thus, such spirits are clothed in white shining raiment, and are remitted into the bloom of their youth, adorned with garlands and celestial decorations (SD 1139-1143).

The Ladder

He has remembered His covenant forever,
The word which He commanded, for a thousand generations,
The covenant which He made with Abraham,
And His oath to Isaac,
And confirmed it to Jacob for a statute,
To Israel for an everlasting covenant,
Saying, "To you I will give the land of Canaan
As the allotment of your inheritance" ... (Psalm 105:8-11).

Angels have no idea of old age, or of the advancing age which is meant by 'coming into days,' but an idea of state in regard to the life in which they are; and therefore when mention is made in the Word of advancement in age, and of old age, the angels who are with man can have no other idea than that of the state of life in which the persons are, and in which men are while passing through their ages even to the last; namely, that they thus successively put off what is human and put on what is heavenly. For human life, from infancy to old age, is nothing else than a progression from the world to heaven; and the last age, which is death, is the transition itself. Therefore burial is resurrection, because it is a complete putting off (AC 3016).

We can all grow younger within while growing older without. The Lord gives us a renewal—a new inner youth—in every stage of life, if we shun the evil that is part of that stage. We can discover heavenly love by discovering the appropriate spiritual love on each successive level: love of obeying, love of others, love of the Lord. Love is not love unless it goes forward into use. The core of use is creativity, which is the heart of being spiritually young.

The life stages are not just internal or abstract; the world has been aware of them for some time:

It is rather humbling to realize that such a view of life as a series of passages, in which former pleasures are outgrown and replaced by higher and more appropriate purposes, was set down in the second century A.D., and it is interesting to compare this ancient Indian concept with ideas about adult development only now evolving in the West. In the first stage described by Hindu scriptures, those gloriously suspended years between the age of eight and the early twenties when one is a student, one's only obligation is to learn. The second stage, its beginnings marked by marriage, is that of householder. The next twenty or thirty years are the time to satisfy the wants of man: pleasure, primarily through family; success through his vocation; and duty through citizenship. When time inevitably dims the pleasures of sex and the senses, when achieving success no longer yields novelty and discharging one's duty has become repetitious and stale, it is time to move on to a third stage: retirement. Any time after the birth of the first grandchild, the individual should be free to begin his true education as an adult, to discover who he is and ponder life's meaning without interruption. Traditionally, people in this stage were encouraged to become pilgrims. Man and wife together, if she wishes to go, were to pull up stakes and plunge into the solitude of the forests on a journey to self-discovery.... The final stage, when the pilgrim reaches his goal, is the state of sannyasin. In the Hindu texts, the sannyasin "lives identified with the eternal Self and beholds nothing else" (*Passages*, p. 515).[3]

Each stage of life has its time of crisis when the choice between aging or growing spiritually younger is made. Isaac's eyes grow dim; Jacob is mistreated by Laban and must separate from him and then wrestle with the angel; Joseph is thrown into the pit, unfairly imprisoned, and endures the famine. It helps in going through them to know that these are not just arbitrary miseries, but a necessary part of evolving to the next level.

The stages and crises of adult life are being studied psychologically, and findings parallel the spiritual level. Erikson noted three major adult stages: "intimacy versus isolation" from ages twenty to forty, "generativity versus stagnation" from ages forty to fifty-five and finally "integrity versus despair."[4]

The idea of "predictable crises of adult life"[5] was brought to widespread attention in Gail Sheehy's book *Passages*. She expanded on Erikson's ideas, preferring the "less loaded word"[6] 'passage' over 'crisis.' Again, there are correlations between stages found in the Writings and those she discovered collecting and analyzing case histories. Her empirical studies divide life into a series of passages. And she includes studies of biological factors that affect these stages, such as menopause and aging.

The stage of "Pulling Up Roots," roughly from eighteen to twenty-two, is the time of leaving the nest and beginning a life of one's own. We "cast about for any beliefs we can call our own.... The tasks of this passage are to locate ourselves in a peer group role, a sex role, an anticipated occupation, an ideology or world view...."[7] This covers 'Ishmael' and early 'Isaac,' the beginning of adult life. 'Isaac' and early 'Jacob' states parallel the next stage Sheehy found:

The Trying Twenties confront us with the question of how to take hold in the adult world. Our focus shifts from the interior turmoils of late adolescence—'Who am I?' 'What is truth?'—and we become almost totally preoccupied with working out the externals. 'How do I put my aspirations into effect?'... Tasks are as enormous as they are exhilarating: To shape a dream.... To prepare for a lifework. To find a mentor if possible. And to form the capacity for intimacy.... Doing what we 'should' is the most pervasive theme of the twenties (*Passages*, pp. 39-40).

The "Catch-30" stage which follows compares with the spiritual stages of Jacob's sons, especially Dan, Naphtali, Asher and Issachar: "a new vitality springs from within as we approach thirty.... Important new choices must be made.... Urge to bust out.... And almost everyone who is married... feels a discontent."[8]

The next passage is "Rooting and Extending," when "Life becomes less provisional, more rational and orderly in the early thirties.... Satisfaction with marriage generally goes downhill."[9] This also reflects the results of 'Jacob's' self-compulsion and the spiritual work represented by his sons. With no spiritual base giving love for 'Rachel,' marriage is likely to become less meaningful as the novelty of the relationship and the insecurities of young adult life wear off.

With the "Deadline Decade" (thirty-five to forty-five) comes a parallel to the separation from Laban:

In the middle of the thirties we come upon a crossroads....
There is grieving to be done because an old self is dying...
reintegration of an identity that is ours and ours alone....
He has been too anxiouy to please.... The man of forty
usuall feels stale, restless, burdened, and unappreciated...
major shift of emphasis away from pouring all their energies
into their own advancement. A more tender, feeling side
comes into play. They become interested in developing an
ethical self (*ibid.*, pp. 43-45).

This new "ethical self" is like Jacob's becoming Israel. The final stage of "Renewal or Resignation" sounds like the rebirth of the natural shown in Israel:

Somewhere in the mid-forties, equilibrium is regained. A new stability is achieved.... These may well be the best years. Personal happiness takes a sharp turn upward.... At fifty, there is a new warmth and mellowing. Friends become more important than ever, but so does privacy...(*ibid.*, pp. 45-46).

All of the eight stages of the life cycle that Erikson noted can be explored in view of the Writings. The infant stage of "trust versus mistrust" (first year of life) can be seen as a time for providing a foundation for loving the Lord. "Autonomy versus doubt and shame" (second and third years) and "initiative versus guilt" (fourth and fifth years), both stages of early childhood, center on giving children a love of truth, of their playmates, and a balanced self-esteem that allows for spiritual growth. Elementary age children face "industry versus inferiority" (ages 6 to 11), a stage which can prepare them for a future use. We have already touched on the stages of "identity versus identity confusion" (ages 12-18), and "intimacy versus isolation" (ages 19/20-40) in earlier chapters. "Generativity versus stagnation" (ages 40-55) covers much of adult life, the fulfilling 'Jacob' years. This leads to the birth of 'Joseph' or spiritual wholeness and the reunion with Esau: "Integrity versus despair" (ages 55 and on).[10] Understanding these psychological stages can enrich our parenting and our own lives.

It is interesting that a key number in the Writings also uses age levels in defining general states, and the parallel between these spiritual states and psychological stages is quite striking.

...from earliest infancy to extreme old age a man passes through a number of states in respect to his interiors that belong to intelligence and wisdom. The first state is from birth to his fifth year; this is a state of ignorance and of innocence in ignorance, and is called infancy. The second state is from the fifth year to the twentieth; this is a state of instruction and of memory-knowledge, and is called childhood and youth. The third state is from the twentieth year to the sixtieth, which is a state of intelligence, and is called adolescence, young manhood, and manhood. The fourth or last state is from the sixtieth year upward, which is a state of wisdom, and of innocence in wisdom... that the first state is a state of ignorance and also of innocence in ignorance is plain.... That the second state is a state in instruction and of memory-knowledge is also plain; this state is not as yet a state of intelligence, because at that time the child or youth does not form any conclusions from himself, neither does he from himself discriminate between truths and truths, nor even between truths and falsities, but from others; he merely thinks and speaks things of memory, thus from mere memory-knowledge; nor does he see and perceive whether a thing is so, except on the authority of his teacher, consequently because another has said so. But the third is called a state of intelligence, because the man then thinks from himself, and discriminates and forms conclusions; and that which he then concludes is his own, and not another's. At this time faith begins, for faith is not the faith of the man himself until he has confirmed what he believes by the ideas of his thought.... From this it can be seen that the state of intelligence commences with man when he no longer thinks from a teacher, but from himself; which is not the case until the interiors are opened toward heaven.... But the last state is a state of wisdom and of innocence in wisdom; which is when the man is no longer concerned about understanding truths and goods, but about willing and living them; for this is to be wise. And a man is able to will truths and goods, and to live them, just insofar as he is in innocence, that is, insofar as he believes that he has nothing of wisdom from himself, but that whatever he has of wisdom is from the Lord; also insofar as he loves to have it so: hence it is that this state is also a state of innocence in wisdom (AC 10225).

It is a wonder of providence that the stages of psychology underpin and support spiritual rebirth. The spiritual teachings deepen and enrich the psychological ideas. It is important to note that the stages of spiritual development are not fixed in terms of years. Jacob, Israel and Joseph states may never be achieved. These spiritual states are distinct from psychological stages. Still, the spiritual promises are there, and they may be built on psychological foundations. There are teachings in the Writings that we will go through major changes of state in our lifetimes, whether we regenerate or not. These 'natural' stages of life come with advancing age, and are inevitable. But they may serve as the basis and foundation for spiritual stages of progress; they strengthen and express interior development. Thus psychological growth and spiritual growth should go hand in hand (cf. AC 5159; and AC 4005, 4136:2; AE 543:3). The general stages of life are relatively self-evident, but on the inner levels—psychological and spiritual—there is much left to be explored:

> It is known that man's state is of one kind in infancy, of another in childhood, and another in youth, another in adult age, and another in old age.... Man puts off his state of infancy with its toys when he passes into the state of youth; that he puts off his state of youth when he passes into the state of young manhood; and this again when he passes into the state of mature age; and at last this state when he passes into that of old age. And if one will consider he may also know that every age has its delights, and that by these he is introduced by successive steps into those of the age next following; and that these delights had served the purpose of bringing him thereto; and finally to the delight of intelligence and wisdom in old age (AC 4063).

Depart in Peace

And behold, there was a man in Jerusalem whose name was Simeon, and this man was just and devout, waiting for the consolation of Israel, and the Holy Spirit was upon him. And it had been revealed to him by the Holy Spirit that he would not see death before he had seen the Lord's Christ. So he came by the Spirit into the temple. And when the parents brought in the Child Jesus, to do for Him according to the custom of the law, he took Him up in his arms and blessed God and said:
"Lord, now You are letting Your servant depart in peace,
According to Your word;
For my eyes have seen Your salvation
Which You have prepared before the face of all peoples,
A light to bring revelation to the Gentiles,
And the glory of Your people Israel" (Luke 2:25-32).

The wise, old Simeon is holding the baby Lord—the secret of everlasting youth—in his arms. He is a leader, recognizing who the Lord is. There are many examples of wise old people in the Word, and as the new age is established, more and more old people will become wise on earth. Instead of being second class citizens, they will be leaders of the heart. Instead of succumbing to narrow and mean qualities, they will be full of gentleness and compassion. They will "dream dreams":

> And it shall come to pass afterward
> That I will pour out My Spirit on all flesh;
> Your sons and your daughters shall prophesy,
> Your old men shall dream dreams,
> Your young men shall see visions;
> And also on My menservants and on My maidservants
> I will pour out My Spirit in those days (Joel 2:28-29).

The "old men" here are the wise and their dreaming dreams means that they instruct concerning truths. These are like the dreams of Joseph, which represent "preaching concerning the Lord's Divine Human."[11] Wise old people can have the depth of experience and integrity to "receive revelation"[12] and to pass on their wisdom—their 'dreams' received from a height of angelic love. This is done not didactically, but rather by their life and love's example, and through open, gentle conversation.

Even now, there are old people who are harbingers of the new age. The uses of older people who have retired from occupations can be the most effective of all. Warmth and faith in the old, who have sustained life's experiences, can touch and uplift at times more than the innocence of an infant. There is something in the innocence of wisdom that touches the true youth in all of us. We can look to the old who are innocent to lead us, especially in things of the heart. The present tendency in the world is to look to youth to lead. But this is because true old age is not as widespread as is ideal. Yet as with conjugial love, its rarity does not mean that it does not exist.

I know one old woman whose sparkling eyes attest to her young spirit. She is avidly interested in people and new ideas, and is still very capable. A few years ago when we were at her house for dinner, my wife was marveling at her abilities as she cooked us a full course meal. She replied: "Yes, eighty-nine years old and I'm still going strong and still have all my marbles!" We all know wonderful people like her who are an inspiration in the face of our own march with time. One minister told me that the senior citizens he gave a class to were the most alive group he ever taught.

With the growth of the new age and the growth of wisdom in old age, death itself will become less and less traumatic, less and less feared. It will be seen again as it was seen in ancient times—as the gateway to heaven and to life. With death, the old body is cast aside and the loving person grows younger until youth in the heart is matched by the beauty of a young spiritual body. Then the angels can say of each of us what was said of Joseph: "Look, this dreamer is coming."[13]

> Those who are in true conjugial love, after death, when they become angels, return to their early manhood and to youth, the males, however spent with age, becoming young men, and the wives, however spent with age, becoming young women. Each partner returns to the flower and joys of the age when conjugial love begins to exalt the life with new delights, and to inspire playfulness.... The man who while he lived in the world had shunned adulteries as sins, and who has been inaugurated by the Lord into conjugial love, comes into this state first exteriorly and afterwards more and more interiorly to eternity. As such continue to grow young more interiorly it follows that true conjugial love continually increases and enters into its charms and satisfactions, which have been provided for it from the creation of the world... Man thus grows young in heaven because he then enters into the marriage of good and truth; and in good there is the conatus to love truth continually, and in truth there is the conatus to love good continually; and then the wife is good in form and the husband is truth in form. From that conatus man puts off all the austerity, sadness, and dryness of old age, and puts on the liveliness, gladness, and freshness of youth, from which the conatus lives and becomes joy (AE 1000).

Chapter 17

The Divine Human

And the Spirit and the bride say, "Come!" And let him who hears say, "Come!" And let him who thirsts come. And whoever desires, let him take the water of life freely (Revelation 22:17).

Conjunction with a visible God...is like beholding a man...on the sea spreading forth His hands and inviting to His arms (TCR 787).

The Divine Human is the one God of creation. He is not some far away and remote Being, an invisible and uncaring Creator. He is Divinely Human, present, and caring—the risen Jesus Christ. Who then is the Father? Philip asked Jesus: " 'Lord, show us the Father, and it is sufficient for us.' Jesus said to him, 'Have I been with you so long, and yet you have not known me, Philip? He who has seen Me has seen the Father.' "[1] And again, Jesus said: "I and My Father are one."[2] The Father, then, is the soul of Jesus Christ! And the Holy Spirit is the uses the Lord does in His creation, looking to save us. So, beautifully, there is one God, and He is Human. "Hear O Israel, the Lord our God is one Lord."[3]

Why are we in the human form? Because we are fashioned in the image of our Creator: "so God created man in His own image, in the image of God created He him; male and female created He them."[4]

The Divine Human means the Lord of creation is a Human Being in form, and, when truly thought of, even in shape and appearance.[5] In a "personal Human form,"[6] He comes right to us and touches us, although it can at times be difficult to see and feel Him closely. To *know* that the Lord is Divinely Human is one thing. To see this, and more importantly, to feel it, is

entirely another. But what is more important than this in life—
to feel the Lord as closely present?

I spoke to a friend in the New Church once about prayer. He
was telling me about how important it was for him to pray and
how vital a doctrine this is, how we don't really use prayer
enough, or correctly. I was very interested and asked him how
prayer actually affected him personally, what it did for him. It
was astonishing to have him say, in almost complete contradic-
tion, that it did not really work for him or help him, and that he
could not find the Lord while he prayed. In fact he hardly felt
any contact with the Lord Himself.

This honesty expresses a problem many of us face. As
Jehovah said to Moses: "You cannot see My face; for no man
shall see Me, and live.... I will put you in the cleft of the rock,
and will cover you with My hand while I pass by. Then I will
take away My hand, and you shall see My back; but My face
shall not be seen."7

It is sometimes disturbing to us that we are told to love a God
we cannot see with our eyes. This lack may even make religion
seem ephemeral—somewhat meaningless in this material
world. Even when our minds are in a state of perception, study
of the Word may not lead us to a direct seeing of the Lord. We
are like Moses, in one small cleft of the rock of truth; when we
would see the glory and warmth of God, instead He covers our
eyes and we see Him only from the back. As Paul said: "We
know in part, and we prophesy in part. For... we can see in a
mirror dimly."8

There are other difficulties in seeing the Lord. We are told
that the Lord is the Word. Yet the Word we see with our eyes is
a book. The Writings are seen by some New Church people as
the Lord speaking directly to us. It is felt that the Lord is directly
present in the series of books that comprise the Writings. How
can we picture the Lord as a series of books? The Writings warn
about thinking too sensually about the Divine Human, and so
we often feel that limiting Him to one picture is too defined and
can lead to over-personalizing and over-sentimentalizing Him.
All this can have the effect of leaving us without a Lord, at least a
Lord we can feel close to, and responsible to, and can love
deeply.

This is not just an intellectual problem. A sense of loneliness and isolation hurts many hearts; many have few close friends. Don't we all need to feel close to God, to seek His warmth and help, and then turn outwards in warmth and help to others? Having a personal relationship with the Lord is essential for spiritual growth. If He is approached with humility, He can become the Comforter within.

One reason the Lord came to earth was so that we can know Him and picture Him. Yet while He was on earth probably no one, except the wise men, knew He was Jehovah incarnate. Not even His mother Mary knew, although "she pondered these things in her heart."[9] His own apostles did not know, except perhaps in fleeting perceptions when He stilled the storm on the sea of Galilee, and when He was transfigured.

It was not until Easter, when the Lord had risen from the tomb, that the amazing truth began to dawn. He appeared in His glorified Divine Human. Finally the realization came— that Jesus Christ is the Lord of all creation! Even Thomas saw it, the doubter who had said: "Unless I see in His hands the print of the nails, and put my finger into the print of the nails, and put my hand in His side, I will not believe."[10] Jesus later appeared before Thomas and said:

"Reach your finger here, and look at My hands; and reach your hand here, and put it into My side. Do not be unbelieving, but believing." And Thomas answered and said to Him, "My Lord and my God!" (John:20:27-28)

Twice the Lord revealed His glorified Human in ways that touch the thought and heart. On the mount of transfiguration, as He prayed with Peter, James and John, "His face shone like the sun, and His clothes became as white as the light."[11] He also appeared to John on the Isle of Patmos:

Then I turned to see the voice that spoke with me. And having turned I saw seven golden lampstands, and in the midst of the seven lampstands one like the Son of Man, clothed with a garment down to the feet and girded about the chest with a golden band. His head and His hair were white like wool, as white as snow, and His eyes like a flame of fire; ... and His countenance was like the sun shining in its strength (Revelation 1:12-16).

In the light of the Writings, we can see the Lord as fully and as convincingly as Thomas did. If our vision is dim, it is because it is obscured by false approaches and false ideas. What can lead us to the true sight of the Lord? "Love of the Lord does not mean loving Him in respect to His person, but it means loving the good that is from Him."[12] When thinking naturally, we tend to picture things in terms of persons, and of what our physical senses apprehend. To think of the Lord from His *qualities first*, and not from His person, may seem abstract—too theological and remote. Yet this is the most real teaching in creation! It is the foundation truth of spiritual perception. It is thinking spiritually, or truly, *into* the natural.

If we really love someone, we think of his or her character first; appearance is secondary. Sometimes we cannot even picture the face of someone we love most tenderly. To love is to love what the person really is—the heart and mind.

> Everyone who thinks of God only from Person, and not from Essence, thinks materially; also he who thinks of the neighbour only from form, and not from quality...(AR 611).

> All who think from themselves or from the flesh about God, think of Him indeterminately, that is, without any determinate idea; whereas they who think of God...from the spirit, think about Him determinately, that is, they present to themselves an idea of the Divine under human form (AC 8705:5; cf. AE 696a:5).

> ...That God is man can scarcely be comprehended by those who judge all things from the sense conceptions of the external man, for the sensual man...think[s]...if God were a man, He would be as large as the universe...(HH 85).

> A master speaking to his boy pupils in the other world said: "Therefore my pupils, think of God from His essence, and from that of His person..." (AR 611).

> The Lord's Human, after it was glorified...[can] be thought of...as the Divine love in human form (AC 4735:2).

With the Lord, His most powerful, tender and gentle love reveals Him—His love and its wisdom. "This is my commandment, that you love one another, as I have loved you."[13] As to quality and essence, He is love itself and thence wisdom itself. Behold the Lamb of God—innocence itself!

This does not mean that He is not a person. We can see that He is, from His birth on this earth and His life's ministry. As the Divine person, He rose from the sepulchre. He is Human in form and shape; we are made in His image.[14] Now He is revealed fully in His Divine Human. These two words, Divine and Human, summarize the whole new doctrine of the Lord: He is Divine as to quality, and this Divine comes to us now in a glorified Human form and shape. All that is truly human—all the qualities and characteristics in our closest friends that are genuine and that we deeply love—these qualities come from His Human. That Human, right with us, is Divine, full of compassionate love and understanding.

The Comforter

But the Comforter, which is the Holy Spirit, whom the Father will send in My name, He will teach you all things, and bring to your remembrance all things that I said to you. Peace I leave with you. My peace I give to you; not as the world gives do I give to you. Let not your heart be troubled, neither let it be afraid (John 14:26-27).

The Lord Jesus Christ is not a book, not even Divine truth by itself. "His eyes were as a flame of fire.... His countenance as the sun shining in its strength."[15] He is the most loving person in creation; it shines in His eyes. The Jesus Christ present in the New Testament is now fully revealed in His Divine nature. He is the "spirit of truth" disclosed in the new Word, that guides to "all truth."[16] Because the Lord is now fully revealed, the New Church is to be "the crown of all churches." The quality now revealed is so beautifully called the "Comforter" by the apostle John.

We so desperately need the Lord's comfort and compassion, His mercy and wisdom in the issues of our lives. How do we find inner happiness in marriage? Why does the Lord permit sickness and tragedies? How are we raised out of our selfishness? How has He ordered creation? What is He truly like in His inmost loves and thoughts? What are His promises to us, in life on earth, state by state? The Comforter reveals answers to these questions in the new Word: in such works as *Conjugial Love*, *The Divine Providence*, *Divine Love and Wisdom*, *The Arcana Caelestia*, and other books of the Writings. Here in tender and gentle terms, rationally unfolded, the Lord speaks right to our hearts. Moreover, He kindles in our hearts a responsiveness to what He says.

He speaks of the nature of true marriage, and its opposite in *Conjugial Love*. In the work on the *Divine Providence*, He treats of the laws governing permissions of evil and tragedy; disclosing how no evil is permitted that will not eventually lead to good. He reveals His own glorification in *The Arcana Caelestia*, and shows how our own rebirth follows the same laws. Creation, its order and subordination to uses, is unfolded beautifully in *The Divine Love and Wisdom*. And the nature of life after death is revealed in detail in the book *Heaven and Hell*.

These truths of the new Word are the "spirit of truth;" and of this Spirit the Lord said: "He shall glorify Me."[17] The Writings are the glory of spiritual truth. They glorify the Lord disclosed in the New Testament! This is why it is said that the "Son of Man shall come in the clouds of heaven, with power and great glory."[18]

The Lord is now fully revealed: His outer and inner nature in the New Testament, and His deeper inner nature in the Writings. In fact, the Old and New Testaments, and the Writings reveal fully the Divine and Human nature of the Lord.[19] The Writings are not abstract rational doctrine far removed from the Jesus Christ of the New Testament. Our inmost remains can perceive that the Writings are Jesus Christ talking directly to our minds and hearts.

As the Divine Human has revealed His qualities fully, showing He is present on every plane of human life, so He can now be received fully on every plane of human life. In the new age a new humanity is possible—people who can receive the Lord more fully and completely. We can now receive Him rationally, naturally, and even sensually—responding on each plane with love. The golden thread can touch each plane with celestial life.

What distinguishes these new human beings? They eat of the tree of life, saying and *believing* that life is a gift of the Lord. They pray for and receive conjugial love, which is eternal and sparkling with warmth and life. They love uses, especially spiritual and celestial uses, and know that heaven is a real and substantial place (state)—the goal of life on earth. All nature comes to sing of its Creator. Gradually, love of others replaces selfishness. They lay down their lives for the Lord, and surprisingly find real life. They are given a strong sense of self-life from the Lord and know this is the gift of gifts. Perhaps there are not many of these angelic beings on earth now, but their numbers will surely grow as the new age progresses.

"He Who Has Seen Me"

He who has seen Me has seen the Father (John 14:9).

How can we picture the Lord? If we think of Him from His qualities of love, innocence and compassion, of wisdom and justice, then a picture will be given to each one of us by Him. We will know and see Him in our hearts in a definite form and shape.[20] When Jesus glorified His body, He became Divinely present in ultimates, able to appear to each of us visibly, adapting our finite idea of Him to show us His glorified, loving person.[21]

We need this ultimate picture of Him; it makes Him Human for us. We may prefer an inner picture drawn for us by Him in His Divine love, or we may want an outward one too. It is needed by our children, and in some form by us. Carvings and paintings of the Lord can adorn our homes and chancels—not to think from these but down into them from His qualities and love. We may want more than one picture, so that our idea does not become so fixed that it cannot grow.[22] There is power in ultimates if the inner love and sight are there. To remove all human form in picturing the Lord in churches and homes tends to remove the truth that He can be approached and worshipped as a person in form and shape.

> If a wise man were to see a picture of one Divine Person with rays of heavenly light about His Head and with the inscription over it, "This is our God, at once Creator, Redeemer, and Regenerator, and therefore the Savior," would not that wise man kiss this picture, carry it home in his bosom, and by the sight of it gladden his own mind, and the minds of his wife and his children...? (TCR 296)

"Inviting to His Arms"

And where I go you know, and the way you know (John 14:4).

To have a true idea of the Lord is first something of the head; to be conjoined with Him is then something of the heart. Alienation, loneliness and the inability to find and love God are things of the heart. What blocks us off from Him?

> To think of God as in a human form is implanted in every man who receives influx from heaven....Those that have rejected influx by self-intelligence prefer an invisible God, while those that have extinguished it by a life of evil prefer no God (HH 82).

If we really need the Lord, He will be there. He appeared to Mary Magdalene first when He rose on Easter morning because she needed His presence. Then He appeared to Peter, who felt unworthy and devastated because he had three times denied the Lord he loved.

Swedenborg went through feeling how unworthy and conceited he was, as he records in the *Journal of Dreams*.[23] It was to this man who felt he was unworthy that the Lord appeared. Swedenborg cried out:

> "And oh! Almighty Jesus Christ, that Thou of Thy so great mercy deign to come to so great a sinner. Make me worthy of Thy grace." I held together my hands and prayed, and then came forth a hand, which squeezed my hands hard. Straightway...I continued my prayer, and said, "Thou hast promised to take to grace all sinners, Thou canst do nothing else than keep Thy word." At that same instant I sat in His bosom, and saw Him face to face: it was a face of holy mien [look], and in all it was indescribable, and He smiled so that I believe that His face had indeed been like this when He lived on earth (*Journal of Dreams* 53-54).

Swedenborg was well prepared for this profound experience. We need to despair over our conceit and pride; the Lord comes to our hearts only if we are in humility.

> Humiliation is the essential of all adoration and of all worship...the Divine of the Lord cannot flow into a proud

heart.... Those who are in humiliation remove themselves
from the Lord, for the reason that they regard themselves as
unworthy to approach the most holy Divine (AC 9377).

"Those who are in humiliation remove themselves from the
Lord." And the miracle is that when they are so removed, from
a deep sense of unworthiness, it is at that very moment that He
comes and lifts them up.

Basically, it is our limited states of heavenly love that block us
off from full conjunction with the Lord. We come near to Him
through the steps of rebirth. As little children, we know and
love Him as our Heavenly Father, feeling His love and protection through our parents. In early adult life, He can come to us
in the beauty of truth; we are aware of Him primarily as the
light of the Word. Later in mid-adult life He may come to us
more closely in our love of the neighbor, when He is felt
essentially as warmth in our love for others. Finally, He may
come right to us, welcoming us at last to His arms, in our
discovery of love of the Lord.

He would always welcome us sooner, but we are usually not
ready, except in states of despair, in temptation, or when we
pray to Him out of spiritual need. His personal presence breaks
through when needed to give peace and hope. A friend of mine
had a fleeting vision of the Lord's face and dreamt of Him
during a time of emotional turmoil. By giving her such powerful and tangible memories to hold onto, the Lord could lead her
gradually into peace. Another friend had a vivid and overwhelming experience of the Lord's love that transformed his
life.

The angels told Swedenborg:

We in heaven say the Lord's prayer daily ... and we do not
then think of God the Father, because He is invisible; but we
think of Him in His Divine Human, because in this He is
visible: and in this He is called by you Christ, but by us the
Lord; and thus to us the Lord is our Father in heaven (AR
839; cf. TCR 113:6).

The mercy of the Lord is universal towards all and each, but
yet is greater towards angels, because they are orphans and
widows—they have no other father nor husband than the
Lord, for they do not trust in themselves (SD 2226).

In infancy the mother and father take the place of the Lord in terms of inmost love. As children grow up, there is a transfer of this tender love away from parents and to the Lord. This is a lifetime process, since earliest remains are in the inmost of the mind, where infantile sensations are allied with the celestial angels and identified with parents. Eventually, there must be a complete transfer to the Lord as the only parent. Our parents become our friends to the degree we can achieve this transfer.

It is said that "the good of innocence of a later state is not to be commingled with the truth of innocence of a former state."[24] In infancy, a truth of innocence is that a parent stands for the Lord. This necessary association is vital in early childhood. It is a truth of a former state. But it is to be replaced in the heart in adult life. The good of innocence then, in this later state, is that the Lord is our Father.

In the New Testament, this is clearly stated by Jesus in talking to the multitudes and His disciples: "do not call anyone on earth your father; for One is your Father, He Who is in heaven."[25] This is openly exhibited in the attitude of good spiritual fathers after death, when they first meet and have a joyous reunion with their grownup children.[26] In this meeting, there is rejoicing if there are good states in each other, and grieving if not. There is delightful conversation on the full reality of eternal life, with its wonder and promise. But when this meeting is over, if internal states are different, then families from earth separate, not in sadness, but with well wishing and rejoicing in the deeply felt truth: ". . . one is your Father . . . in heaven." This loving Father is Divine love and Divine wisdom in His very present Human.

Like the angels, we may come to be "orphans and widows," not in a devastating sense, since parents are still loved, but in a beautiful, liberating sense. Tender and gentle loves we felt for our parents are then transferred to their true origin.

The negative feelings of emotional disorders can also be projected onto the Lord. Children who are rejected by their parents can feel rejected by the Lord, and transfer their anger towards the parents to the Lord also. He can be unconsciously felt as untrustworthy or secretly cruel. This is counterbalanced by the celestial remains of loving the parents. Seeing the transference of hate or fear to the Lord and acknowledging it, and removing these negative things from Him, helps in seeing Him as He truly is—love itself, gentleness itself, and wisdom itself. The pain and sorrow of parental rejection can be replaced by a deep love and trust of the Lord. A secret helper in this is the spiritual 'mother' of human life, the inmost celestial heaven. This heaven gives the golden thread that leads to the Lord.

The Lord becomes a person then, most close, and loneliness and alienation leave our hearts. He holds us in His arms, as He held Swedenborg.

Knowing that this conjoining is a gradual process can give us patience while being faithful. Little by little we draw near Him. How is this done? I suggest six approaches:

1) *Read the Word.* By means of the Word there is "conjunction of heaven with the world and thus of the Lord with man."[27] The Lord is not a book, but He is the Divine Truth, that is, it is from Him and so is He.[28] The Word elevates us above sensuous spheres and into the light of heaven.[29] "The Word conjoins man with the Lord .... Man has life by means of the Word."[30]

2) *Keep the Commandments.* "If you keep My commandments, you shall abide in My love."[31] As adults, we can perceive that the Word is the Lord's; then love is shown by the willingness to compel ourselves to obey Him. We realize that much in our hearts and thoughts is still unregenerate, cutting us off from the Lord.[32] But loyalty through self-compulsion will lead to Him.

3) *Perform an occupation faithfully and honestly.* Through occupation, the Lord leads into regeneration, and the discovery of spiritual use. Use expresses love of the Lord above all else.[33] John the apostle represents such love of use, and that is why "the Lord loved him more than the rest... because he represented uses."[34]

4) *Receive the Holy Supper (communion).* He comes to us, and conjoins Himself with us, when we come to the Holy Supper with genuine preparation. This means we give up merit, and ascribe all that is good and true to the Lord. "The

193

SPIRITUAL HEALTH: SIX APPROACHES

1 - Read the WORD

2 - Keep the COMMANDMENTS

3 - Perform an OCCUPATION faithfully

4 - Receive the HOLY SUPPER

5 - PRAY

6 - Take the time to be HAPPY

whole of the Lord, and the whole of His redemption, are present in the Holy Supper. He is present as to the glorified Human, and as to the Divine from which the Human is."[35]

5) *Pray.* "Prayer . . . is speech with God . . . . If man prays from love and faith, and for only heavenly and spiritual things, there then comes forth in the prayer something like a revelation (which is manifested in the affection of him that prays) as to hope, consolation, or a certain inward joy."[36] Through prayer, we can talk to the Lord directly. And we need this—to talk to the person we love the most.

6) *Take time to be happy!* We are allowed to step back from the hurry of life, and to reflect upon the beauty of the Word, and its astounding promise of eternal life in heaven. The deep contentment in this can come down, and make all nature alive as the work of the fingers of God, the Divine artist. It is right to take time to be happy in the beauty of the Lord in creation and in His promise of life forever in heaven.

The Lord so loves the human race, and each of us, that it is beyond our comprehension. He found His "inmost joy" in knowing that His glorified Divine Human would be the means of saving the human race.[37] Our idea of the Lord qualifies everything in our life. Because He glorified His body, He can appear alive and *visible* to our finite minds. He conjoins Himself with us by "putting on something finite, and thus by accommodation to reception."[38] We worship a Divinely Human Lord who loves us and invites us to His arms.

And I saw a new heaven and a new earth, for the first heaven and the first earth had passed away. Also there was no more sea. Then I, John, saw the holy city, New Jerusalem, coming down out of heaven from God, prepared as a bride adorned for her husband. And I heard a loud voice from heaven saying, "Behold, the tabernacle of God is with men, and He will dwell with them, and they shall be His people, and God Himself will be with them and be their God. And God will wipe away every tear from their eyes; there shall be no more death, nor sorrow, nor crying; and there shall be no more pain, for the former things have passed away" (Rev. 21:1-4).

Notes and References

PART I: MENTAL HEALTH
CHAPTER 1: INTRODUCTION: WHICH SELF

1. Nathaniel Branden. *The Psychology of Self-Esteem* (Bantam Books, Nash. Ed., L.A., 1969).
   Robert Ringer. *Looking Out for Number One* (Funk & Wagnalls, NY, 1977).
   Dr. Wayne Dyer. *Pulling Your Own Strings* (TY Crowell Co., NY, 1978).
   Theodore Mischel. *The Self: Psychological and Philosophical Issues* (Blackwell, Oxford, 1977).
   Nathaniel Branden. *Honoring the Self: Personal Integrity and the Heroic Potentials of Human Nature* (JP Tarcher, L.A., 1983).
   Theodore Rubin. *Compassion and Self-Hate* (D. McKay Co., NY, 1975).
   R.D. Laing. *The Divided Self: an Existential Study in Sanity and Madness* (Tavistock Publications, London, 1969).
2. Erik Erikson. *Identity and the Life Cycle* (W.W. Norton & Co., Inc., NY, 1968).
3. Dr. Leo Buscaglia. *Love* (Fawcett Crest Books, NY, 1972) Chapter 6.
4. English versions of Swedenborg's Writings use the term 'man' as a translation of the Latin 'homo,' which refers to either sex.
5. Emanuel Swedenborg. *Conjugial Love* (CL) (The Swedenborg Society, London, 1978), #35, 36 Translation by Alfred Acton.
6. Emanuel Swedenborg. *Angelic Wisdom Concerning the Divine Providence* (DP) (Swedenborg Foundation, Inc. New York, 1941), Chapter 1.
   Emanuel Swedenborg. *Arcana Coelestia* (AC) (Swedenborg Foundation, Inc. New York, 1949), Volume 5, #3993:8-13.
7. Emanuel Swedenborg *On the Divine Love and on the Divine Wisdom* (DLDW), (Swedenborg Society, Inc., London, 1963). DLDW refers to a manuscript of two parts titled *Concerning the Divine Love and Concerning the Divine Wisdom*. It is a separate manuscript from the work Swedenborg published later, entitled *Angelic Wisdom Concerning the Divine Love and Wisdom*. We quote from the 1942 translation by the Rev. E.C. Mongredien published by the Swedenborg Society. The Swedenborg Society first published this translation in 1942 under the title *Doctrine of Uses*. In the Swedenborg Foundation publications, it is found bound in with the final volume (VI) of the *Apocalypse Explained* under the titles of "The Divine Love" and "The Divine Wisdom" (Swedenborg Foundation, Standard Edition, 1949, translation by John Whitehead). The DLDW we use as a reference is

197

according to the numbering given by the Rev. E.C. Mongredien, but he also includes the Roman numeraling, as given in the Swedenborg Foundation translation, #40.

8. See Rt. Rev. George de Charms. *Growth of the Mind* (Academy Book Room, Bryn Athyn, PA, 1953), Chapter 6.

9. Cf. re "heaven of human internals" AC:7270:2-4, AC 1999:3.

10. *The Holy Bible*, New King James Version. (Thomas Nelson Publishers, Nashville, Tenn., 1982), John 8:36. All Biblical translations are taken from this translation. Some changes have been made in wording when the internal sense revealed in the Writings indicates a different translation from that given in the New King James.

11. Emanuel Swedenborg. *Posthumous Theological Works*, vol. I (Swedenborg Foundation, Inc., New York, 1947), Coronis 29.

12. The 'Word' is the canon of the New Church, and includes all those works in the Bible which have a continuous internal sense. Other books of the Bible are of great value, but lack that Divinely written correspondential format that conjoins the Lord and heaven with us when we read the Word reverently. The books of the Word are given in "The New Jerusalem and Its Heavenly Doctrine" from Swedenborg's *Miscellaneous Theological Works* (Swedenborg Foundation, Inc., NY 1941), #266.

13. Emanuel Swedenborg, *Arcana Caelestia* (AC) (The Swedenborg Society, London, 1983). Quotations from Volume I of the *Arcana Caelestia* (#1-1113) are taken from this new translation by John Elliot, #129.

14. Cf. DP 227.

15. Emanuel Swedenborg. *The Spiritual Diary* (SD) (James Speirs, London, 1883), #3474.

16. M.Scott Peck. *The Road Less Travelled* (Simon and Schuster, New York, 1978).

17. John 14:6.

18. Mark 5:4.

19. Emanuel Swedenborg. *Heaven and Its Wonders and Hell* (HH) (Swedenborg Foundation, Inc., New York, 1964), #14.

20. The Lord's Divine nature is the origin of the masculine and the feminine, although in its oneness of love and wisdom it is above the terms masculine and feminine. He is tenderness and love itself, the first origin from which is the feminine. He is wisdom itself, the first origin from which is the masculine. The term 'He' is used because Divine love is seen through Divine wisdom, but both are wonderfully and warmly His One nature.

21. Emanuel Swedenborg. *The True Christian Religion* (TCR) (Swedenborg Foundation, Inc., New York, 1949), #475.

22. Cf. DP 42, 210, et alia.

23. AC 1661.

24. Matthew 13:30.

25. AC 4063:2,3.
26. See Rev. Geoffrey S.Childs. "Mediate Good" *New Church Life* (General Church of the New Jerusalem, Bryn Athyn, PA, 1960), pp 222-231, 270-279.
27. AC 3701:4.
28. AC 5353.
29. Luke 15:17-19.
30. Cf. DP 277a:1.
31. Revelation 2:7.
32. Emanuel Swedenborg. *The Apocalypse Revealed* (AR) (Swedenborg Foundation, Inc., New York, 1947), #89.
33. See Rt. Rev.George de Charms. *The Doctrine of the Proprium* (General Church Publication Committee, Bryn Athyn, PA, 1962), especially pp 9-13.
34. TCR 43.
35. DP 42, 210, 29:4, 76, 129, 116, et alia. Some other references on the self and mental health: Dr. Hugo Odhner. *The Human Mind* (Swedenborg Scientific Assoc., Bryn Athyn, PA, 1969).
Erik H. Erikson. *Identity, Youth and Crisis* (WW Norton & Co., Inc., NY, 1968).
Carl G. Jung. *The Undiscovered Self* (Little & Brown, Boston, 1958).
Erich Fromm *Psychoanalysis and Religion* (Bantam Books, 1950).
Wilson VanDusen. *The Natural Depth in Man* (Swedenborg Foundation, Inc., NY, 1971), and *The Presence of Other Worlds* (Swedenborg Foundation, Inc., NY 1974).

CHAPTER 2: THE GOAL AND THE SETTING

1. AC 16.
2. William Shakespeare. *Hamlet*, Act IV, Scene 5.
3. DP 27.
4. John 15:12.
5. Revelation 1:18.
6. John 11:25.
7. TCR 29:3, DLW 93-98, and HH 116-125.
8. HH 120, AC 7270:2-4, 8443, 1999.
9. AC 1999.

CHAPTER 3: AND HE BLESSED THEM

1. DLDW 75.
2. DLDW 82.
3. AC 5052:3, 5054.
4. DLDW 82.
5. Frederick Leboyer. *Birth Without Violence* (Random House, New York, 1975).
6. AC 1410-1414.

7. DLW 270, TCR 417.
8. Rt. Rev. Nathaniel D. Pendleton *Glorification* (Academy Book Room, Bryn Athyn, PA, 1941), p.7.
   Emanuel Swedenborg *The Apocalypse Explained* (AE) (Swedenborg Foundation, Inc., New York, 1928), #314:3.
9. Cf. AC 8443, 7270:2-4.
10. AC 8443, 7270.
11. Op. Cit., Leboyer, Pt. I, p. 1.
12. AC 3183:1.
13. HH 408e.
14. DLW 270, AC 1428, 1893 et. alia.
15. CL 396.
16. HH 14. Cf. AC 4906, 5071, 6032, 6314.
17. Op. Cit. Leboyer, p. 74 et. alia.
18. Isaiah 11:6.
19. John 1:29.
20. AC 10134:2.
21. Luke 2:7.
22. Luke 2:11-12.
23. DLDW 75.
24. AC 1100.
25. HH 341.
26. AC 5125e.

CHAPTER 4: STORGE

1. *Oxford Universal Dictionary* (Oxford University Press, London, 1955), p. 2031.
2. Luke 15:24.
3. CL 396, 393.
4. Emanuel Swedenborg. *The Apocalypse Explained* (AE) (Swedenborg Foundation, Inc., New York, 1946), #710:2.
5. HH 278.
6. Luke 1:38.
7. CL 396.
8. CL 405.
9. AC 1555.
10. Cf. AC 1947.
11. Matthew 12:48-50.
12. Psalm 68:5-6.

CHAPTER 5: EMOTIONAL DISORDERS

1. CL 392.
2. DP 141.
3. Cf. DP 141.
4. John 16:13.

5. SD 5709.
6. Cf. DP 141.
7. See Chapter 6 ("Which Self?") for further explanation of these terms.
8. DP 141.
9. Alfred Acton (translator and editor). *Letters and Memorials of Emanuel Swedenborg* (Swedenborg Scientific Association, Bryn Athyn, PA, 1955) p. 696.
10. DP 141.
11. HH 14.
12. AC 8164.
13. DP 141.
14. SD 2715, 2603.
15. Matthew 2:18.
16. Psalm 36:9.
17. AC 5386.
18. SD 734; cf. AC 2693.
19. John 14:6.
20. HH 225.
21. HH 14.
22. AC 3993:9-11.
23. Op. Cit. Acton.
24. AC 8164.
25. DP 141.
26. AC 8164.
27. AC 8164e.
28. Ibid.
29. DP 281.

CHAPTER 6: POSSESSION?

1. HH 257e.
2. Mark 5:5.
3. Wilson VanDusen. "The Presence of Spirits in Madness," (Swedenborg Foundation, Inc., New York, 1978). This is a chapter from his book *The Presence of Other Worlds* (Swedenborg Foundation, Inc., NY, 1974).
4. AC 2535.
5. DP 133.
6. HH 250.
7. SD 3624.
8. Ibid.
9. Cf. AC 8164.
10. Cf. AC 741, 840.
11. Exodus 14:15.
12. AC 8609.
13. Matthew 22:37-39.
14. AC 8611.

CHAPTER 7: HEALING IN HIS WINGS

1. DP 282.
2. DP 181.
3. AC 2693, SD 734, et alia.
4. Genesis 21:17.
5. AC 2693.
6. AC 3471.
7. Mark 5:20.
8. DP 320.
9. HH 14.
10. Jeremiah 33:6.
11. DP 141.
12. John 13:7,8.
13. DP 111.
14. CL 7.
15. Ibid..
16. HH 399.
17. DLDW 43.
18. CL 249.
19. Ibid..
20. AE 1194.
21. DLW 336. For further reading on uses: Wilson Van Dusen, *Uses: A Way of Personal and Spiritual Growth*, Swedenborg Foundation, Inc., NY, 1978).
22. DLDW 43.
23. Ibid..
24. John 14:2.

PART II: SPIRITUAL HEALTH

CHAPTER 8: THE DIVINE PROMISE

1. DP 27.
2. Hosea 14:7.
3. TCR 650.
4. Ibid..
5. Ibid..
6. TCR 651.
7. HH 358.
8. Genesis 37:19.
9. Cf. AC 8164e.
10. Cf. SD 5709, 5710.

CHAPTER 9: ABRAM AND CHILDHOOD

1. Genesis 12:5.
2. AC 1438.

3. Genesis 12:7; cf. AC 1445.
4. AC 1419.
5. Cf. DP 275.
6. AC 4063:1-5.
7. AC 4063:4.
8. AC 4563:2.
9. DP 277a:4.
10. SD 6051.
11. AC 1661, 1670 et alia.
12. HH 318.
13. HH 329e; ital. added..
14. AC 5236.
15. TCR 652.
16. AC 1456-7.
17. AC 1561.
18. Ibid..
19. Cf. AC 1495, 1461-2, 1472, 1475.
20. Maya Pine "Launching Healthy Children" *Life Magazine Special Report* (Time-Life, NY, 1971).
21. AC 1452:1.
22. Matthew 18:2.

CHAPTER 10: ABRAHAM AND ADOLESCENCE

1. Although the Writings use the term *adolescentia* to cover a wider age range, our definition is "the period of life between puberty and maturity," *Webster's New School and Office Dictionary* (Fawcett Crest, NY, 1974).
2. Genesis 14.
3. Genesis 14:4.
4. Genesis 14:18.
5. AC 1724.
6. Cf. AC 1724-1738.
7. Genesis 15:1.
8. Cf. AC 1810, 1808, 1805-7.
9. Matthew 6:33.
10. AC 2222.
11. AC 1838-1857.
12. CL 64.
13. AC 2039.
14. AC 2004.
15. AC 2010.
16. Erik Erikson. *Identity, Youth and Crisis* (WW Norton & Co., Inc., NY, 1968).

CHAPTER 11: ISHMAEL: THE BIRTH OF REASON

1. Genesis 16:6.
2. Genesis 16:10.
3. AC 1896.
4. AC 1895.
5. AC 1949.
6. Genesis 17:20.
7. AC 1895.
8. AC 2657:2.
9. Ibid..
10. TCR 508:3.
11. AC 2568.
12. CL 31.
13. William Durant. *The Story of Philosophy: the Lives and Opinions of the Great Philosophers* (Simon & Schuster, NY, 1961), Francis Bacon, First Aphorism of *Novum Organum*.
14. AC 1495:2.
15. Genesis 21:18.
16. AC 2699.
17. Genesis 3:5.
18. Matthew 28:6.

CHAPTER 12: THE COVENANT WITH ISAAC

1. Genesis 17, 18.
2. Genesis 18:11.
3. Genesis 21:6.
4. AC 2638.
5. Cf. AC 2083.
6. AC 2072.
7. AC 2083, cf. AC 2066, 1899, 2063, et alia.
8. AC 2496.
9. Genesis 24:50.
10. AC 2039.
11. CL 305.
12. Ibid..
13. CL 312.
14. CL 460, AC 9182-9184.
15. Revelation 8:5.
16. AE 491.
17. AE 489:2a.
18. Genesis 1:27.
19. CL 32.
20. Genesis 1:26.
21. CL 305.
22. CL 302.

23. CL 137.
24. CL 115.
25. CL 127.
26. CL 115.
27. AC 2039.
28. Cf. AC 2034:7.
29. John 4:10, 14.
30. Genesis 27:1.

CHAPTER 13: JACOB'S BLESSING

1. AC 3508, 3518.
2. AC 3576:2.
3. John 14:15; ital. added.
4. Genesis 25, 27.
5. Cf. HH 528, 530.
6. Genesis 29:11.
7. Genesis 29:18.
8. Genesis 29:25.
9. Genesis 30:22.
10. Genesis 31:2.
11. AC 4286, 4292.
12. AC 4336-4373.
13. AC 4592, 5411, 5413; SD 4640; AE 449 et alia.

CHAPTER 14: ASCENDING AND DESCENDING

1. Genesis 29:31.
2. AC 3855.
3. Genesis 49:2-3.
4. Genesis 49:4.
5. AC 3913:4,5; 3901-4038.
6. AC 3913:5.
7. AC 3925.
8. AC 3924.
9. Genesis 49:21.
10. AC 3925.
11. AC 3934:2,7.
12. CL 68.
13. CL 59e, 68.
14. AC 3939, 3937.
15. AC 3938, 3926, Genesis 30:13 and AC 3939.
16. Anne Morrow Lindbergh. *Gift from the Sea* (Pantheon Books,NY, 1975-25th anniversary printing).
17. AC 6201:2.
18. Hugo L. Odhner. *The Divine Allegory* (Swedenborg Foundation, Inc., NY, 1954), p. 110.

19. Cf. TCR 652:3.
20. Cf. AC 1937, 1947.
21. Psalm 68:27.
22. Deuteronomy 33:12.
23. AC 4592:6.
24. AC 5469.
25. *Liturgy and Hymnal* (General Church of the New Jerusalem, Bryn Athyn, PA, 1966), p. 579. Based on Numbers 24:5.
26. AC 2568.
27. AC 3236:2, 3207:5; AE 707, 708; TCR 787; HH 79; AR 611.

CHAPTER 15: "THIS DREAMER IS COMING!"

1. AC 5332.
2. Genesis 37:24.
3. John 9:25.
4. AC 5077:3.
5. DP 100-128.
6. AC 1616:4.
7. Cf. AC 5078, 5869, 5877-5885, 5926-5931.

CHAPTER 16: GROWING YOUNG

1. HH 414.
2. Isaiah 40:1.
3. Gail Sheehy. *Passages: Predictable Crises of Adult Life* (Bantam Books, NY, 1977), p. 515.
4. Op. Cit. Erikson. *Identity, Youth and Crisis*, p.94, etc.
5. Op. Cit. Sheehy, subtitle.
6. Ibid., p. 23.
7. Ibid., pp. 37-39.
8. Ibid., pp. 41-43.
9. Ibid., p. 43.
10. Op. Cit. Erikson. *Identity, Youth and Crisis*, Chapter 3.
11. AC 4682.
12. AE 624:8.
13. Genesis 37:19.

CHAPTER 17: THE DIVINE HUMAN

1. John 14:8-9.
2. John 10:30.
3. Deuteronomy 6:4.
4. Genesis 1:27.
5. AC 7211.
6. Coronis 48.
7. Exodus 20-23.
8. I Corinthians 13:9,12.

9. Luke 2:19.
10. John 20:25.
11. Matthew 17:2.
12. HH 15.
13. John 5:12.
14. AC 7211, AR 839, AC 8760:2.
15. Revelation 1:14,16.
16. John 16:13.
17. John 16:14.
18. Matthew 24:30.
19. Cf. TCR 109:2, AC 4211:3.
20. Cf. AC 7211, AR 839, AC 8760:2.
21. AC 8760:2.
22. Cf. HH 55.
23. Emanuel Swedenborg. *Swedenborg's Journal of Dreams, 1743-1744* (Swedenborg Foundation, Inc., NY, 1977).
24. AC 10681, 9301, 3519:7.
25. Matthew 23:9.
26. CL 406.
27. HH 258.
28. John 1:1.
29. Cf. AC 6201.
30. Emanuel Swedenborg. *The Four Doctrines* (Swedenborg Foundation Inc., NY, 1949), "Doctrine of the Holy Scripture," #3. Cf. AE 1111, AC 4867, SD 6025. Cf. re "White Horse" Revelation 19:11, AR 820-828.
31. John 15:10.
32. AC 1937.
33. DLDW 35-40, AC 7038.
34. AC 7038.
35. TCR 716.
36. AC 2535, cf. AC 10299; AE 248:4, AR 278, AC 8179, 6619; AR 376.
37. AC 2034.
38. AC 8760:2.